POLLUTION CONTROL IN

POLLUTION CONTROL IN A DEVELOPING ECOMOMY

A Study of the Situation in Ghana

by

S. B. AKUFFO
Managing Director, Goodwill Associates Limited, Accra
Formerly Research Officer, Environmental
Protection Council, Accra

GHANA UNIVERSITIES PRESS
ACCRA
1989

Published by

Ghana Universities Press
P. O. Box 4219
Accra

ISBN: 9964–3–0165–0

PRODUCED IN GHANA
Typesetting by MES Equipment Limited, Accra
Printing and Binding by Assemblies of God Literature Centre Ltd., Accra

To

Nana Kwasi Akuffo
My Grandfather who was the Paramount Chief
of Akuapim 1895–1907 and 1920–1927

CONTENTS

Preface

Chapter

TABLES

Table

FIGURES

ACKNOWLEDGEMENTS

I wish to express my sincere gratitude to the following who read through the original manuscript and made various corrections and suggestions. Dr. R. B. Turkson, Faculty of Law, University of Ghana, Legon; Mrs. Justina R. Anipa, Town and Country Planning Department, Accra; Mr. George K. Akosah, Faculty of Engineering, University of Science and Technology, Kumasi; Dr. W. R. Phillips, Chemistry Department, University of Ghana, Legon; Mrs. Irene Amissah, West Africa Examinations Council, Accra; Mr. D. A. Seidu, Bank of Ghana, Accra; Mr. J. S. Martinson, Mobil Oil Ghana Ltd., Accra; Mr. J. K. Danso, Environmental Protection Council, Accra; Mr. K. A. A. de Graft Johnson, Mr. Charles Biney, Institute of Aquatic Biology, Accra and Mr. Edward Akwagyiram, Business Consultant, Hasted Ltd., Accra.

I am also very grateful to Mr. Denison Adja Torgbor, my very reliable Typist who did all the typing. Finally, but not the least I wish to express my fondest appreciation to my wife, Mrs. Elizabeth Akuffo, of Ebenezer Secondary School, Accra for her encouragement and support.

PREFACE

it properly. It becomes a problem it, after reaching its final stage of disposal, it creates any of the problems mentioned above. Well-managed cities and industrial establishment may

Many decades ago when life in Ghana, formerly Gold Coast, was predominantly rural and the population small, a book of this nature would not have been necessary. Resources were bountiful and people, at that time, lived within the capacity of the environment to sustain them. With the advent of modern civilization, however, things have changed drastically. There has been a rapid population increase due mainly to improved health facilities. There is also increased urbanization and industrialization.

A large number of people have moved from rural areas to urban centres in pursuit of jobs and better conditions of life. This has resulted in the springing up of unplanned sections in the urban centres with slums and insanitary conditions.

The situation in the country has been made worse by the apparent lack of co-ordination among organizations whose activities affect the environment. This brings about isolated and unco-ordinated projects on the environment especially in health and in sanitation. Such projects are funded rather sporadically and can hardly fit into a properly-managed environmental development process. They do not, therefore, make any positive impact on the declining environmental conditions. It is thus quite clear that unless Government elects to enter environmental operation at the planning level and adopt a "total environment approach" to development, the decline will continue culminating in intractable pollution problems.

Pollution is a term generally applied to the introduction into the environment of substances which are either harmful to human health, resources and the ecosystem or which impair the legitimate use of the environment. These uses which are many and varied include economic, social, cultural, aesthetic and amenity uses.

Pollution is very much associated with urbanization and industrialization and it is at times confused with sanitation. In order to ensure smooth administration of the two problems we need to distinguish between them. Sanitation may be defined as the arrangement to get rid of filth from immediate human surroundings so as to prevent the spread of diseases. Waste remains a sanitation problem so far as there is an opportunity to collect and dispose of it properly. It becomes a pollution problem if, after reaching its final stage of disposal, it creates any of the problems mentioned above. Well-managed cities and industrial establishment may, therefore, not have sanitation problems but they may pose serious pollution problems. Thus, there is the adage that "pollution begins where sanitation ends". Although solution to sanitation problems may not provide solution to pollution problems, the establishment, use and maintenance of infrastructural facilities for sanitation management provides the basis for pollution control.

The scope of this book is limited to pollution problems which arise out of the normal domestic, industrial and agricultural activities associated with everyday living in a developing country. Specifically, it deals with air and water pollution control and the administration of toxic chemicals. It does not discuss such international problems as the depletion of the ozone layer due to the use of certain chemicals especially chlorofluorocarbons (CFC) or the "Greenhouse effect" due to the increase in concentration of carbon dioxide in the atmosphere. It does not also discuss the intentional or accidental discharges of large volumes of pollutants into the environment. Intentional discharge such as the use of chemicals for fishing and unauthorized dumping of hazardous wastes are straightforward criminal offences which are normally dealt with under the criminal code and through international co-operation. Accidental discharges such as the Chernobyl nuclear disaster and oil tanker accidents are normally dealt with under industrial safety regulations and also through international treaties and conventions.

I have restricted myself in this way because I believe pollution problems associated with everyday living are those problems the solution of which lies entirely, or at least should be so, within the competence of most developing countries. This is also the area where solution has become very elusive to managers and policy makers in many developing countries. It is, therefore, the area where, I believe, a serious start should be made.

Pollution control and environmental management in general are major aspects of development processes and no nation can afford to neglect them for any length of time. The cost of such neglect is quite tremendous. It is, therefore, quite essential for planners and decision makers to appreciate the need to look at development from a broader perspective, in terms of sustained development of human well-being in its entirety and the preservation of the environment for posterity. The parochial view of development only in terms of per caput income, number of cars, houses, TV sets per family etc, completely disregarding damage caused to the environment, is clearly unacceptable. What perhaps sustains this parochial view is that pollution is very much associated with what might be termed economic and industrial progress. This makes it difficult for industrialists and traditional economists to see pollution for what it is; "where there is smoke there are jobs" they may say. To them, spending money on pollution control may constitute investment without return and may also be a major cause of inflation. There are others, however, who hold the other extreme view that, with industrial pollution, industries should be made to pay the full cost for rendering harmless all effluents they produce as obtains in certain cases in the developed countries. These two view-points are rather extreme if pollution control is to be taken seriously in a developing country.

A significant view-point and a middle-of-the-road approach relevant to the situations in many developing countries was expressed by W.T. Slick Jr, a Senior Vice President of Exxon Corporation. He says "Environmentalists must hold themselves accountable for the cost and possible broader impact of their actions on the economy and the nation just as the public and the private sectors must be held accountable for their actions on the environment". This view-point is expressed rather differently in the following thesis which serves as a criterion for the determination of environmental standards in Britain: "Pollution should be abated to the point where extra benefit to society from further abatement just equals the extra cost to society of this abatement". These view-points can serve as useful guidelines for the promotion of a healthy growth in a developing economy, where the sentimentalist view of pollution control (preservation) cannot be allowed to stem industrial and economic progress, neither can industrial and economic progress (exploitation) be allowed to erode the quality of the lives of the people and the wholesomeness of the environment. The delicate balance that ought to be maintained between economic and industrial progress on the one hand and the need to maintain environmental quality on the other (conservation) requires a thorough understanding of the problems involved, highly-trained professionals to be in charge of environmental management affairs and suitable institutional arrangement made for the purpose.

In spite of much efforts and good intentions on the part of planners and decision makers in many developing countries, the apparently low level of understanding of the basic principles of pollution control in these countries has made it difficult to chart this delicate course in order to achieve the desired goal. Although many excellent books have been written on the subject of pollution and its control, most of these books were written with the problems of advanced countries in mind. Discussions in them are, therefore, at levels and in context that leave managers and decision makers in many developing countries unguided and confused as to how to approach the problem. It is, therefore, my intention to try and explain, in this book, the complexities and the principles involved to a broad spectrum of our people: managers, decision makers, economists, engineers, planners, students in various sectors of environmental operation etc., using Ghana's experience, so as to help them make the best use of available resources for the sustenance of a dignified life.

Accra
6th June, 1986   S.B. AKUFFO

Chapter 1

URBAN GROWTH PROBLEMS

Introduction

In many developing countries, the development of basic infrastructural services such as water supply, sewerage and other sanitation facilities lag far behind urban growth. Coupled with this, there has been inadequate control of urban growth and urban management. These factors create problems for the maintenance of safe minimum standards of environmental quality in the urban environment.

One of the main reasons for urban growth problems in developing countries appears to be that development planning has not been comprehensive and adequate provisions have not been made for project co-ordination and for the sustained singleness of purpose for the stable continuation of project managment. Another reason has been inadequate financial resources in these countries, which tends to force the people to place subsistence high above environmental quality. Thus, all available resources are channelled into, what is considered as, more immediate productive ventures. This attitude, however, brings about the perpetuation of the poverty conditions, for it is known that places with improved environment and efficient services attract more investments.

This chapter examines urban growth problems as they exist in the Accra Tema Metropolitan Area of Ghana, and provides the basis for the discussion of pollution control policies and pollution control legislations in Chapter 2 and Chapter 3.

The Accra Tema Metropolitan Area (ATMA), the study area, consists of Accra, the capital of Ghana, and Tema, the major sea port of Ghana. It stretches from the Greenwich Meridian (longitude 0°) at Tema to longitude 0° 13" West in Accra. It also lies on latitude 5° 35" North.

Up to 1948, Tema was a fishing village with a population of about 10,000. In the 1950s, a new township with a deep sea port was built to replace the old township. The new township has developed into a major industrial centre.

Accra started as a small fishing village in the 16th century and has developed into a major metropolis. It has an industrial area mainly bordering the Korle Lagoon at the centre of the city. Unlike Tema, which is planned, many parts of Accra have not been planned. They have rather grown around a pattern of villages and old settlements characterized by poor-quality buildings and congestion. Living conditions in the unplanned areas are made worse because water supply, sewerage and refuse disposal facilities have not been adequate. These problems have attracted considerable attention of planners and decision makers in the past, but the situation remains largely unchanged.

In the early 1960s, the Government of Ghana commissioned the preparation of a comprehensive master plan for the development of the ATMA (Doxiadis, 1962). Following the plan, the Government established a single municipal authority to administer the area. Large-scale developments were envisaged for the central area between Accra and Tema, and it was expected that Accra and Tema would be fully built up by the 1980s. The services which were considered for the area at that time were based on this plan (Tahal, 1981). The plan was, however, largely not followed especially in Accra where spontaneous developments have characterized the sprawl in many parts of the city. Some of the unplanned spontaneous-growth areas are Nima, Maamobi, Alajo, Abeka, Darkuman and Sukura in Accra, and Ashiaman, a suburb of Tema. These areas are heavily congested with buildings and structures and a high percentage of houses are only accessible through rain-rutted alleys (Fig. 1).

The Town and Country Planning Ordinance of 1945, which is the current law on urban growth and urban management, has for several decades not been enforced. Many developers, therefore, build on reservations for roads, drains, public toilets, markets, school, parks and gardens etc., thus throwing the plan out of order and creating slums and insanitary conditions.

Some governmental projects also went contrary to the plan in the early stages of its implementation. For example, whilst it was expected that developments, both housing and industrial, would take place east of Accra, where facilities had been concentrated, the Dansoman housing estate project undertaken by the State Housing Corporation appeared on the western side of Accra where

2

Fig.1 Rain-rutted alley in Accra New Town (a suburb in Accra) (*Picture by Dan Offei*).

water and electricity supplies have not been adequate. The plan was further set back when, in 1974, a new Local Government system was established with separate District Councils for Accra and Tema.

Population

Population in the area in 1984 was 1,155,415 consisting of Tema population 190,526 and Accra population 964,789. (Census, 1984). Population growth rate in the area has been very rapid especially after independence (1957) in Accra and during the rapid industrialization in the late 1950s and early 1960s at Tema (Tables 1 and 2). In general, however, one would not say that the area is heavily populated. Tall buildings are scarce, and tall residential buildings hardly exist. The problem, however, is the unbalanced distribution of population especially in Accra. The density distribution in Accra is closely related to the standard of living, the poor areas being densely populated. The less dense areas, up to 150 persons per hectare, cover 86 per cent of the land and accommodate only 49 per cent of the population. The remaining 14 per cent of land house 51 per cent of the population. (Table 3).

One of the major causes of rapid population increase in the poor areas has been the lack of controls which brings about the high incidence of spontaneous developments. It has not been easy either to control the movement of the poor and desperate people into these areas. The Nima-Maamobi area is typical. It covers about 190 hectares and has a population of 80,000. This represents 9 per cent of the Accra population whilst the housing stock of 2,300 represents only 4 per cent reflecting a high housing occupancy (Huszar Brammah and Associates 1977).

Infrastructural Services

Water Supply

There are two sources of water supply for the area: the Kpong Water Works, about 60 km north of Tema, treats water from the Volta River and the Weija Water Works, about 20 km west of

4

TABLE 1

Population of Accra since 1891

Year	Population	Average Growth Rate
1891	16,000	–
1901	27,000	5.4
1911	30,000	1.1
1921	44,000	3.9
1931	61,000	3.3
1948	136,000	4.8
1960	388,000	9.1
1970	636,000	5.1
1984	965,000	3.0

Source:

Tahal Consulting Engineers Ltd., Tel Aviv, Israel 1981. *Final Report ATMA Water Supply and Sewerage Project. Review of the Master Plan,* Vol. 1; *1984 Population Census of Ghana.*

TABLE 2

Population in Tema since 1948

Year	Population	Average Growth Rate
1948	10,000	–
1960	28,000	9.0
1970	102,000	13.8
1984	190,000	4.6

Source:

Tahal Consulting Engineers Ltd., Tel Aviv, Israel 1981, *Final Report ATMA Water Supply and Sewerage Project Review of Master Plan,* Vol. 1; *1984 Population Census of Ghana.*

TABLE 3

Population Density Distribution in Accra

(Based on 1970 Census Data)

Persons/Hectare	Per Cent Land	Per Cent Population
Less than 50	55	15
50 – 150	31	34
150 – 250	8	18
250 – 350	2	7
350 – 500	2	9
More than 500	2	17

Source:
Tahal Consulting Engineers Ltd., Tel Aviv, Israel 1981. *Final Report ATMA Water Supply and Sewerage Project, Review of Master Plan,* Vol. 1.

Accra, treats water from the Densu River. Production figures in 1980 were Kpong 190,680 m^3/day and Weija 60,000 m^3/day (Tahal, 1981).

Water consumption in the area is very much determined by the way it is obtained (Table 4). In Tema (except Ashiaman and Tema Manhean area), every household has a house connection and water-closet type of toilet, but in Accra about 70 per cent of the population fetch water by house or yard connection whilst the rest fetch water from public stand pipes or neighbourhood vendors. Again, only 30 per cent of the houses in Accra have water closet. The other 70 per cent use pan and public pit latrines and others (Table 5).

Improving this level of service is a major problem for policy makers, for it will require considerable amount of investment not only to improve the supply of water but also to carry out urban renewal in most of the congested areas. The dense and often irregular pattern of buildings in these areas will make it extremely difficult to construct water mains and sewers in the narrow passages and lanes between the dwellings. In Nima, for example, it

6

TABLE 4

Mean Domestic Water Consumption per
Caput by Source of Water

Source	Mean Consumption	
	Litres/Day	*Gals/Day*
House connection	137	30.1
Yard connection	85	18.6
Public stand pipe, neighbourhood vendors etc.	30	6.6

Source:
   Tahal Consulting Engineers Ltd., Tel Aviv, Israel 1981. *Final Report ATMA Water Supply and Sewerage Project Review of Master Plan,* Vol. 1.

has been estimated that the best level of service that could be provided under the present conditions would be yard connection for 20 per cent of the houses and public stand pipes for the rest.

The planning of water supply for the area has not been easy for two main reasons,

   (a)   There is virtually no information on the permitted population densities for various parts of the area.

   (b)   There is no master plan indicating expected areas of population increase.

These factors have made it extremely difficult to make accurate forecast for water demand. For these reasons, wide-range of forecasts regarding future water demand has been made for the area.

It has been assumed that there will be a gradual improvement in the present level of service over time in Accra (i.e. from 70 per cent house or yard connection in 1980 to 80 per cent in 2010). With this in mind, Tahal (1981) made three population projection

7

TABLE 5

Type of Sanitary Facility Utilized in Accra
(Per cent of Households Surveyed)

District	Does your house have its own toilet?			What type of toilet does your household use?			
	In the house	Yes In the yard	No	WC	Pan	Public Pan Public Pit	Other
1. James Town *	56.0	12.0	32.0	–	62.0	38.0	–
2. Ussher Town *	32.2	–	67.8	–	29.5	69.8	0.7
3. Adabraka *	34.0	59.6	6.4	21.3	72.3	6.4	–
4. Korle Gonno *	16.9	63.9	19.3	10.8	69.9	16.9	2.4
5. Mamprobi	15.8	54.7	29.5	12.6	49.5	25.3	12.6
6. Sabon Zongo *	–	–	–	–	–	–	–
7. Abossey Okai *	65.4	28.8	5.8	11.5	75.0	13.5	–
8. Kaneshie *	91.2	6.5	2.2	84.8	8.7	1.1	5.4
9. Kokomlemle *	64.0	25.0	11.0	34.0	54.0	12.0	–
10. Accra New Town	50.0	35.2	14.8	4.5	71.6	7.4	16.5
11. Nima **	39.5	23.3	37.2	34.9	27.9	37.2	–
12. Cantonments	91.7	8.3	–	79.2	20.8	–	–
13. Osu *	96.6	1.4	–	69.4	30.6	–	–
14. Labadi	88.5	3.3	8.2	18.0	77.0	4.9	–
15. Teshie	45.5	2.7	51.8	0.9	45.5	32.1	21.4
16. Nungua and Eastern Outskirts	97.3	0.9	1.8	85.0	12.4	2.7	–
17. Northern and Western Outskirts	61.6	30.6	7.8	9.1	54.3	14.2	22.4
18. Tema	100.0			100.0	–	–	–
19. Tema New Town (Manhean), Ashiaman	26.9	17.3	55.8	7.7	34.6	50.0	7.7
20. Oblogo ***	–	13.0	87.0	–	8.7	21.7	69.6
Total	58.8	21.3	19.9	30.2	43.7	17.9	8.1

Notes on Table 5

*   Area covered by Contract S/1 sewerage system*

**   Only one enumeration area was taken in Nima; and examination of the original reply forms shows that 15 of the 45 questionaires were for Kanda Estate which is a medium grade area; this is where the WC's would be. There are very few in the traditional Nima portion:

*** Rural village included for comparison purposes

Source: Tahal Consulting Engineers Ltd, Tel Aviv, Israel *Final Report ATMA Water Supply and Sewerage Project. Review of Master Plan,* Vol.2.

assumptions to provide the basis for estimating water demand (Fig. 2) up to the year 2010:

(a) Low population projection: natural increase plus 5 per cent in-migration rate.

(b) Most-likely population growth projection: natural increase plus 11 per cent in-migration rate.

(c) High population growth projections: natural increase plus 20 per cent in-migration rate.

The demands estimated under these assumptions show considerable range: 650,000 m³/day for alternative (a) and 1,450,000 m³/day for alternative (c) (Fig.3). It has, therefore, been suggested that to keep variations within reasonable limits, the water supply facility incorporated in the master plan (Tahal, 1981) would be carried out in stages, each stage being adapted to the actual population growth and water demand trends as they develop with time. This certainly is not an easy task for it will require Ghana Water and Sewerage Corporation (GWSC) to keep vigil and to execute their work well in the midst of uncontrolled urban growth.

Under the 1980 production capacity, which stands at about 245,000 m³/day, about half of the population of Accra do not receive regular supply of water. Some of the problem areas are: South Odokor, Dansoman, Sukura, Tesano, Abeka, Teshie, North Kaneshie, Bubuashie, Darkuman, Madina, Legon and Pantang.

9

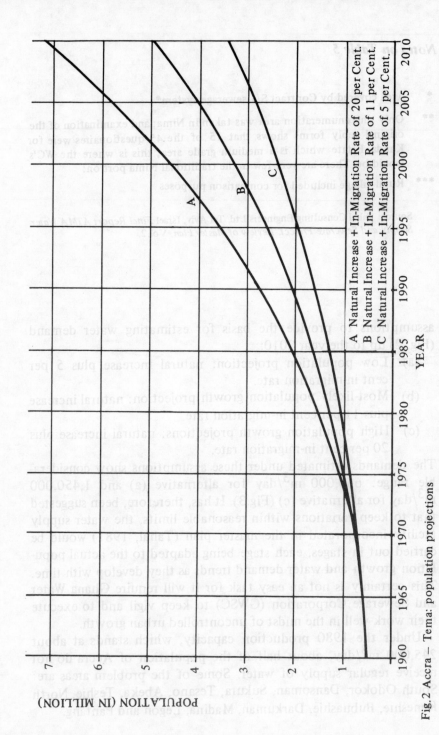

Fig.2 Accra – Tema: population projections

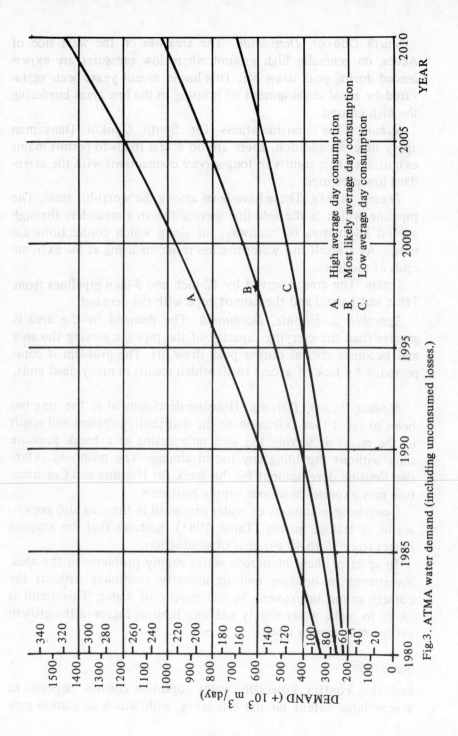

Fig.3. ATMA water demand (including unconsumed losses.)

A. High average day consumption
B. Most likely average day consumption
C. Low average day consumption

11

South Odokor, Dansoman. The area lies on the west side of Accra, on generally high ground where low pressures are experienced during peak draw off. This has in recent years been aggravated by rapid development of housing in the low areas bordering the high ground.

Sukura. The considerations for South Odokor Dansoman apply here. In addition, there are no access roads to permit mains extensions. This results in long-service connections with the attendant low pressures.

Tesano, Abeka. These have been among the worst-hit areas. The pipeline which is the sole line serving the area meanders through several kilometres of roadway, all along which connections are made. As a result, no water reaches residents living at the extreme ends of the line.

Teshie. The area is served by 12-inch and 9-inch pipelines from Tema and Labadi and the cannot cope with the demand.

Kaneshie, Bubuashie, Darkumah. The demand in the area is greater than the carrying capacity of the pipeline serving the area and becomes critical during peak draw off. The problem is compounded by lack of access roads which results in many dead ends.

Madina, Legon, Pantang. Housing development in the area has been so rapid that extension to the distribution system will result in the reservoir serving the area only acting as a break pressure tank without providing any useful storage. The proposed extensive housing development by the Bank for Housing and Construction may experience serious supply problems.

Considerable amount of water produced in the area also goes to waste. A leakage survey (Tahal, 1981) indicates that the amount ranges from 30 to 40 per cent of production.

In spite of these numerous water supply problems in the area, investment in housing and in industry continues without the corresponding investment in the supply of water. This trend is likely to make water supply a serious limiting factor in the growth processes sooner or later.

Sanitation

Pollution control, especially water poplution control, depends to a very large extent on the efficiency with which sanitation pro-

12

blems are handled. This is especially so in a developing country where most of the pollution load comes from domestic rather than industrial sources. The neglect of sanitation makes it almost impossible to control pollution because waste has to be effectively collected and treated before it is discharged to avoid pollution.

In the rural areas, the very dispersal of people is a powerful factor in reducing pollution problems due to insanitation. Here, individual efforts are sufficient for the efficient management of waste. As the size and the concentration of community grows, there comes a stage where individual efforts no longer suffice. At this stage, public funds have to be committed in a planned and sustained manner for the provision, operation and maintenance of infrastructural facilities for sanitation management.

In the study area, the lack of co-ordination among organizations whose activities affect the environment and the debility of law enforcement have together made sanitation an intractable problem. Two other powerful retrogressive factors have been the lack of maintenance consciousness among the citizens and the desire for temporary solutions.

Some of the relevant bye-laws whose enforcement have become laxed are the Cleansing Bye-laws of 1975 and the Removal of Night-Soil Bye-laws of 1975.

The Cleansing Bye-Laws of 1975. These laws forbid the putting up of unauthorized structures, posters and hoardings. They also forbid the throwing of litter into gutters and drains. In spite of these provisions, numerous unauthorized structures have sprang up in recent times in the area especially in Accra. Car workshops and garages have sprung up everywhere and abandoned cars and scrap metal make the city look unsightly. Coupled with these is a great deal of commercial activities in unauthorized places. These activities leave considerable amount of filth in gutters and drains.

The Removal of Night Soil Bye-Laws of 1975. These bye-laws deal with night soil collection. There is also provision that all house owners in the area, covered by the contract S/1 sewerage system in Central Accra should provide water closets in their premises a year after coming into force of the bye-laws. A survey conducted in 1980 (Table 5) shows that considerable number of houses in the area still use pan latrines showing noncompliance with the bye-laws. Some of the problems with the implementa-

13

tion of this provision have been:

   (i) The practical difficulty of introducing water closets into the congested areas covered by the system;

   (ii) The high cost of connecting to the system; and

   (ii) The inadequate water supply to provide for such a high level of service.

Refuse management is an area where the problem is quite considerable. There are about 130 official communal refuse dumps in Accra and about 10,000 dustbins at private houses (Tahal, 1981). The dustbins serve only 4 per cent of the population whilst the rest are expected to take their refuse to communal dumps. The number of official communal dumps is, however, small and this has led to the creation of about 100 more unofficial dumps. Refuse from these unofficial dumps seldom gets collected. There is also wide-spread dumping of refuse in stream as well as in water channels which pass through the town. In the congested areas, the large open drains provide the only available space for the dumping of refuse. One of the worst areas where this can be seen is at Nima, through which the Odaw stream passes (Fig. 4). When the rains come, most of the refuse are washed into the Korle Lagoon, the beaches and some also litter the streets.

Stagnant waters which are formed behind refuse dams in these water channels have become breeding grounds for mosquitoes and malaria is becoming more highly endemic over ever widening area. Ironically, malaria control with prophylactics always assume greater importance than mosquito control programmes through efficient waste water management. This is but fighting the shadow and not the substance. The relationship between refuse management and public health needs no emphasizing. The problems created by pests, particularly flies and mice have become very serious in the study area.

In the congested areas, some dumping sites are used as playgrounds by children, and also for indiscriminate defaecation, and for the dumping of uncollected night soil. The indiscriminate defaecation is due mainly to inadequate toilet facilities in these areas. The situation is worsened by the fact that, many landlords in the areas have converted their toilets and kitchens into living rooms for hiring. Many tenants, therefore, have to use the beaches and the dumping grounds for defaecation. Landlords in these

14

Fig. 4. The Odaw stream at Nima (a suburb of Accra) being used as refuse dump. (Picture by Dan Offei).

15

areas are now being encouraged to put up 'Kumasi Ventilated Indirect Pit' (KVIP) latrines, a variation of the Reed Odourless earth closet developed at the University of Science and Technology in Kumasi. This type of latrine, however, appears more suited for rural locations (Tahal, 1981) and urban fringes rather than for congested areas in the cities.

In the Nima-Maamobi area, there are only 8 public toilets of the aqua privy type and a very high average of 400 persons per hole has been estimated . To improve upon this situation it has been suggested that about 60 toilets with 24 units per block will be required. This will provide an average of 50 persons per hole. The problem is, however, lack of space for such a bold plan. The area is fully built up and the available space is even less than sufficient for pedestrian circulation (Hussar Bramah and Associates, 1977). A comprehensive redevelopment with appropriate resettlement is perhaps the most reasonable solution. However, such resettlement projects can hardly be accommodated in the present budgetary allocation. Worst still, the trend in deterioration continues and many newly developing areas are fast degenerating into conditions found in the slums.

Sewerage Systems. On sewerage systems, Tema provides a lead. The new development at Tema was provided with modern sewerage facilities and this has continued with the continual expansion of the town except in Ashiaman and the Tema Manhean areas. Tema, of course, is the only city in the country which is completely sewered. However, the sewerage system deals only with domestic wastes which are discharged untreated into the sea through an outfall. Inspection of the three pumping stations of this sytem showed, however, that they were all seriously affected by lack of adequate maintenance (Tahal, 1981). At the pumping station No. 1, only one pump out of the three installed was in working condition. At the pumping station No. 2, none of the three pumps was working and at pumping station No. 3 only two out of four pumps were working. In none of the cases was the flow recorder operating properly. Industrial wastes on the other hand are discharged into open channels which empty into the Chemu Lagoon and finally into the sea near the fishing harbour where the effects have become marked and objectionable even at the present low industrial output (Fig. 5).

Fig. 5 / Chemu Lagoon at ebb tide exposing the filth underneath. (Picture by Dan Offei).

In Accra, there are eighteen sewerage sytems and sewage treatment plants serving some institutions, but none of them is operating or being maintained in accordance with the designers intentions (Tahal, 1981). The conditions of the plants at Burma Camp, Korle Bu Teaching Hospital and the University of Ghana are described below:

The plant at Burma Camp is the largest individual plant in the study area. It serves a population of about 25,000 mainly military personnel and their families. The plant is of the trickling filter type and is followed by a stabilization pond, from which the effluent discharges into a water course leading to the Kpeshie Lagoon. Inspection of the sedimentation tanks showed that they have not been disludged for a long time. The top of the tanks is filled with a crust of sludge of considerable thickness in which grass and weeds grow. The flow now by-passes the bacteria beds and is led to a single stabilization pond which has been constructed a little further down the stream valley.

The treatment plants at the Korle Bu Teaching Hospital are of the trickling filter type, and the associated pumping stations are now effectively inoperative and have been so for a long time, the flows going into the Korle Lagoon untreated. In 1975, a 38.10cm diameter intercepting sewer was constructed by the State Construction Corporation (SCC) in order to divert the flow to the newly-constructed Korle Bu pumping station and thence into the new sewer system constructed under Contract S/1. However, the quality of sewer laying was so poor and infiltration into the new sewer so great that the Ghana Water and Sewerage Corporation (GWSC) refused to allow it to be connected to the pumping station.

The pumping station at the University of Ghana, Legon and to which the south side of the Legon Hill University Campus drains has been inoperative for sometime, because of lack of spare parts for the pumps and motors. Thus, the flow, instead of being pumped over the brow of the hill to the sewage treatment works which lie some 1500 metres north of Legon Hill, now flows into the pumpwell and then out again, via an emergency overflow, into the nearby water course. The pumpwell acts, therefore, as a septic tank of inadequate size.

The sewage treatment works which is of the trickling filter

type is in grossly neglected condition; no maintenance appears to have been carried out on equipment, units or the grounds for a very long time (Fig.6).

One major drawback for the efficient operation of these plants is that they are under the control of organizations (Military Authorities, Hospitals, Schools etc.) whose primary functions are not to manage waste, and there is virtually no supervision on these plants. Waste is something that nobody wants except, of course, when it becomes a resource. So if its management is placed under an organization whose primary function is not to manage waste, it easily gets neglected.

The GWSC has been given powers to take over these small works (Legislative Instrument 1233, 1979) but none of them has been taken over. The only sewerage system under its control is the Contract S/1 sewerage system in Central Accra. This system which discharges sewage untreated into the sea was designed on the assumption that both foul sewage and sullage would be taken into the sewers. However, the sub-standard housing and the overcrowded accommodation in the poor areas served by the system make it difficult for plumbing standards to reach the requirements for greater proportion of sullage to be admitted into the system. Also the cost of constructing a toilet in the poor areas (where this is possible) and connecting it to the sewer is often beyond the means of the inhabitants. The sewerage system is, therefore, heavily under utilized.

In the original Master Plan prepared in 1965, most of the congested areas were taken into consideration as regards sewage flow they would generate after redevelopment. However, due to the socio-political problems associated with uprooting a substantial population from their homes, the current policy in the reviewed plan is to adopt appropriate technology to deal with health and sanitation problems in the sub-standard areas.

Meanwhile, the bulk of waste water in the city, both domestic and industrial, continues to be discharged into gutters and drains and most of which empties into the Korle Lagoon in the centre of the city. The lagoon is in a sorry state. The Biochemical Oxygen Demand (BOD) can be as high as 300—400 mg/1 at certain parts and a terrible stench emanates from it especially during the dry

19

Fig.6 A Biological filter sewage treatment plant at the University of Ghana, Legon. (The rotating arm has been stationary for many years with sewage oozing out from the sides of the stationary centre pillar). *(Picture by Dan Offei).*

season. Excreta and refuse are also found stranded at the high tide line. (Fig.7).

On sewage treatment, stabilization ponds have been suggested as being the most appropriate since they do not rely on extensive electro-mechanical equipment and also that they are easy to construct and operate (Tahal, 1981). However, due to lack of space for their construction, it has been suggested that direct sea outfall without treatment would be the correct ultimate solution, although the construction of a sea outfall will involve the expenditure of a considerable amount of foreign exchange. The sea does not have an infinite capacity to absorb waste material, but it is nevertherless a valuable treatment resource just as land and river. This resource should, however, be used responsibly. At present, the oil pipe line donated by the Mobil Oil Company which was used as an outfall for the discharge of sewage from the contract S/1 sewerage system is now in such poor condition that it is effectively out of commission. This has led to the discharge of raw sewage from the main pumping station just at the beach, worsening the already deplorable state of the beaches in the area.

This deplorable state has been created largely by the nightsoil tipping station in the area. Cesspool emptiers and pan trucks discharge their content into an old thinly concreted sloping area. Workers apply water from hoses to the material and with aid of brooms wash the nightsoil down the slope onto the beach to be carried away by the tide. Most of the nightsoil are, however, deposited along the beach. The tipping station has operated in this crude and unhygienic fashion for many years.

Other Essential Services

In the area, there has been the tendency for planners and decision makers to plan for and build "super" structures for markets, banks, post office, etc., at few places whilst many areas lack these facilities (Fig. 8). Everyday, people troop to a few places to obtain essential services. Such invitation to congestion at few places creates considerable problems for the efficient management of these facilities. Our marketing practices, especially food marketing, produce a great deal of filth and, with such congestion, waste

21

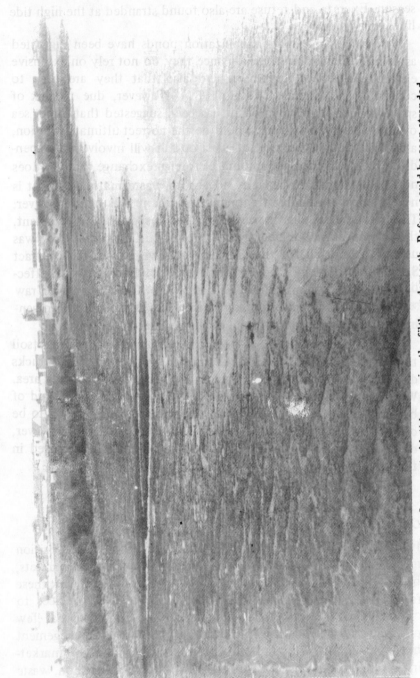

Fig.7. Korle Lagoon at ebb tide exposing the filth underneath. Refuse could be seen stranded at the high tide line. (*Picture by Dan Offei*).

Fig.8. A huge market complex at Kaneshie a suburb of Accra. (Many areas in the city lack the facility. As seen from the picture much of the trading activities take place not inside the market but on the pavements by the sides of a busy trunk road. The situation presents considerable danger to all and sundary).(*Picture by Dan Offei*).

management becomes an almost impossible task. It is certainly a better policy to make every community within the city self-sufficient in terms of essential services to reduce congestion, the movement of people and the problems that go with them. People should not be forced to travel over great distances to reach their objectives at the expense of their most precious leisure time. Moreover, it is far cheaper to transport goods and services than to transport people.

If the desire is to beautify the metropolis with high-ranking buildings, investment could be directed into such facilities as hotels, musuems, conference centres, theatres etc. but not into markets, banks and post office which are meant to provide essential services.

Open Spaces and Green Belts

The principle of creating open spaces is very much lacking in the area. Worst still, already-existing open spaces are encroached upon by powerful developers both private and governmental and the area, especially Accra, is fast becoming one solid mass of buildings.

In most well-managed cities about a third of the built-up area is left as open spaces. Admittedly, in most developing countries people object far less to the environmental pressures of crowding. But to promote efficient waste management and to improve the welfare of the people, a certain minimum spacing and spaces are desirable. The motive is to offer a decent and respectable entertainment to the urban worker family. As written by William Moris in 1887, "Our towns must not eat up the fields and natural features of the country; nay I demand even that there be left waste places and wilds in it or romance and peotry which is art will die amongst us".

The area is also not delimited by any green belts and there is uncontrolled expansion. This does not allow for the design and construction of water supply and other facilities that cannot easily be overloaded.

When considering the problems of settlement, it should be realized that towns that are built now will continue to exist for centuries to come and should, therefore, be planned in such a way as to ensure that the basic infrastructural facilities are well taken care of and that there is provision for the unobstructed and independent extension of such facilities. Some components such as houses and their facilities may be done away with within one or two generations, but the basic frame should last for several generations and perhaps centuries. To what extent can we say this is true of the study area and do we fully appreciate the problems and the dangers inherent in the present trends?

Sources of Air Pollution

In the study area, some of the major sources of discharges into the atmosphere are:
(1) Aluminium smelter palnt at Tema.
(2) Brick and tile manufacturing plant in Accra.
(3) Oil refinery at Tema.
(4) Fuel combustion and exhaust fumes from motor vehicles.
(5) Dust from Tema Cement Works and dust from Volta Aluminium Company's (VALCO) installation at the Tema Harbour.
(6) Generation of Smoke.

Aluminium Smelter Plant

Aluminium smelting causes the emission of fluoride gases. Whilst a few milligrammes per litre of fluorides are beneficial to animals, higher levels produce symptons of fluorosis. Airborne fluoride gases are usually not in sufficient concentrations to affect animals directly. However, farm animals can be poisoned by fluoride residues that have been deposited from air on vegetation.

Brick and Tile Manufacturing Plant

Brick and tile manufacturing also produces fluorine and sulphur compounds. At present, no practical economic process has been found for removing sulphur and fluorine compounds. The practice has, therefore, been to build higher chimney stacks to disperse the gases into greater volume of air for greater dilution to reduce their concentration on the ground. Modern chimney stacks are normally over 122.00m high. In spite of this, certain climatic conditions such as a severe inversion can concentrate the pollutant on the

25

ground.

Oil Refinery

Oil processing always produces such gaseous compounds as sulphur dioxide (SO_2), sulphur trioxide SO_3) and also hydrogen sulphide (H_2S). Sulphur dioxide and sulphur trioxide dissolve in water to form sulphurous and sulphuric acids. Hydrogen sulphide is also oxidized in air to form sulphuric acid. In Europe and other industrialized areas where a large number of oil processing plants are located and where large quantities of coal and fuel are burnt, the concentration of these gases in the atmosphere is quite high and this has resulted in acid rains. This causes a lot of damage (corrosion) to property and also affect fauna and flora in many rivers and lakes. Human beings are also affected by low concentration of these gases especially sulphur dioxide and also hydrogen sulphide.

Fuel Combustion and Exhaust Fumes

Fuel consists mainly of carbon and carbon compounds. In an unlimited air supply, fuel burns off to give mainly carbon dioxide, a colourless odourless gas which is harmless. However, in case of limited supply of air, incomplete combustion occurs leading to the formation of carbon monoxide. This is a highly toxic gas which is freely absorbed through the lungs and combines strongly with haemoglobin to form carboxyhaemoglobin. This compound shows little tendency to combine with oxygen, and the blood loses its capacity for transporting oxygen to the tissues. The inhalation of air containing 1000 mg/1 of carbon monoxide quickly leads to inactivation of haemoglobin and rapid death due to anoxia.

Carbon monoxide is released from vehicle exhausts. It is less dense than air and disperses quite rapidly after emission. Nevertheless, higher levels can exist locally over considerable period when the gas is being continuously liberated. This can happen in enclosed spaces such as garages and sometimes in open air during traffic jams. In Accra, there are always heavy traffic jams during certain periods of the day at the city centre and other places. People, especially anaemic people, with low haemoglobin levels are likely to suffer from dizziness, headache, lassitude and other symptoms of poisoning if the concentration of carbon monoxide goes high enough. To alleviate this problem may require the

26

redesigning of road networks and the redistribution of services to ease congestion.

Dust Sources

In the study area, there is always some amount of dust in the air caused by vehicular movement on untarred portions of roads and through wind action on dusty grounds. At Tema, additional source of dust has, on some occasions, come from the Tema Cement Works and VALCO installations at the port. These companies have responded quite promptly to some of these discharges in the past. However, it is hoped that in the future they will pay more attention to maintenance of equipment to prevent the occurrence of such discharges rather than to take corrective measures after they have occurred.

Smoke Sources

The generation of smoke in the area is on the increase. Smoke from the growing traffic due particularly to worn out engines is on the tremendous increase. Other sources of smoke are from singeing of skins of sheep and goats and from the burning of refuse, especially in unauthorized refuse dumps, where refuse collections have been very irregular if ever they are carried out.

Chapter 2

APPROACHES TO POLLUTION CONTROL

Basic Principles

Pollution control policies and legislations in any country must relate to the level and the operational efficiencies of the environmental management technologies existing in that country as well as to the socio-economic conditions in the country. If this does not happen, there might be situations where there are nice pollution control laws on the statute books which cannot be implemented. In other words, pollution can be controlled only to the extent feasible.

There are basically two approaches to pollution control, the various blends of which are found in many countries. These are:

(1) Best Available Technology Approach.

(2) The Best (Reasonably) Practical Technology Approach.

The Best Available Technology Approach

Under the Best Available Technology (BAT) Approach, the idea is to make use of the best technology available on the world market for development process including waste management processes. The aim here is to ensure the highest efficiency in the use of resources and also the highest quality of effluents discharged from trade premises and sewage treatment plants. This approach does not usually take into consideration the assimilative capacities of the receiving media for the effluents. In places where the environment is not grossly polluted and/or the economy not strong enough, therefore, it may have the disadvantages of being unduly restrictive and economically burdensome in many instances. Many developing countries can, therefore, hardly afford the cost of such technology. Uniform standards are also implied under this approach and this may provide incentive for continuing to locate industries at worst possible sites from the environmental point of view. However, in the advanced countries and in industrialized areas where finance may not be a limiting factor and where the rivers and the environment in general are grossly polluted, it may be the best approach to ensure a reasonably clean environment. Again in a situation where pollution directly affects public health, as it is with the discharge of asbestos dust into work environment, financial constraint may not be accepted as a limiting factor. Here the BAT approach may have to be adopted in both developed and developing economies.

The Best Practical Technology Approach

The Best (Reasonably) Practical Technology (BPT) approach is normally adopted where financial resources are limited, especially as in devloping countries, and it is based on the maintenance of a delicate balance between,

(a) the ability of the nation, industries and the individuals to pay for pollution control facilities, and

(b) the need to maintain at least minimum standards of environmental quality in relation to the requirements of public health and also the health of the environment.

The basic aim here is to pursue the least costly way of cleaning the environment and to avoid the pursuit of idealistic maximum standards, inherent in the BAT approach, which may produce economic dislocation in various sectors of the economy.

The question that needs to be answered here is not whether a nation can afford pollution control facilities, but whether it has the facilities at the level that it can afford. With efficient controls in urban growth and urban management and with a total environmental planning approach to development, it is possible to provide these facilities at sufficiently high level and also at a reasonable cost. But this is where the problem lies in many developing countries as shown in Chapter 1. Due to its relevance to problems in developing countries, the BPT approach will be examined in greater details.

Most planners and decision makers who disregard environmental parameters in the development process in these countries are often far removed from the consequences of their decision and from the people who suffer from them. It is always the urban poor people, for example, who suffer from improper planning and poor implementation of plans that bring about slums and insanitary condi-

29

tions. There are some people who argue that pollution control can be postponed until a country's economy is reasonably bouyant and in the position to afford it. If this line of thinking is accepted, the problem would become increasingly more complicated and also too difficult to solve in the future. This is borne out by the numerous socio-economic and technical problems facing the authorities in their attempt to re-develop some of the slum areas in the cities. In developing a nation, unlike solving mathematical problems, the traditional oriental view that "the reality of the whole is greater than the sum of the parts" is always a better guide. As development proceeds so must the basis for sound environmental management be created. Nations need both development and a clean and healthy environment. For this reason, the sole aim of environmental policy must not consist in the removal of damage to the environment once it has occurred which is rather very expensive. Efforts must rather be made through comprehensive and co-ordinated approach to development to prevent such damage from the beginning or to reduce it to a justifiable degree.

The absence of comprehensive and co-ordinated approach in the development processes in Ghana has and continues to create a lot of problems (*See* Chapter 1). Another example involving industrial development is found at Cape Coast in the Central Region. Some years ago, an area was zoned as industrial area. No drainage or sewerage systems were provided for the area and yet the authorities started issuing licences to industrialists to start establishing factories there. A soap manufacturing industry was the first to be established and when it started operation, the factory's effluents collected in large pools in the area creating odours and considerable nuisance. Residents in the area started complaining bitterly, but nothing could be done, for without waste management facilities in the area, the factory could not do much about the effluents. The alternative was to have asked the factory to close down, but nobody dared ask for that. Soap is an essential commodity in the country and as such a suggestion like that would not be entertained in any quarters. Some people argued that the factory could be asked to recycle its effluents to reduce the pollution load. Yes, that could be done, but the factory itself might undertake that action without any promptings from environmentalists if the economics of it were right. There are situations where there could be tax incentives or reliefs for industries to undertake such actions to promote environmental quality. But this should not overshadow the fact that certain essential waste management facilities should have been provided to allow the industrial concerns to operate as viable enterprises. Meanwhile, the situation persists and the cost of providing the facilities keeps on mounting.

There are some people who also feel that with industrial pollution, industries should be held fully responsible for rendering harmless all the effluents they produce as obtains in certain cases in the developed countries where, unlike the developing countries, closing down one or two factories may have little effect on their economies. Even in the developed countries, certain serious problems are taken as national problems rather than a problem for industries. For example, when detergents were introduced after the Second World War, and received world-wide acceptance because, unlike soap, they were not affected by the hardness of water, they created a lot of problems because they were partially biodegraded at sewage works and final effluents from such works contained enough detergents to give rise to foaming in streams and rivers. This created a great deal of nuisance and affected dissolved oxygen (DO) levels as well as the ecology of these rivers.

The immediate reaction was not to ban these detergents which had proved to be very useful nor to ask industries to bear the full responsibility for rendering them harmless. In Britain, for example, a technical committee was set up to study the problems and to provide solutions.

Experimental work carried out (Hammerton, 1955) showed that the resistance of these detergents to biological breakdown was due to the structure of the alkyl group present in the molecule. Detergents such as Teepol containing straight-chain alkyl group, eg $CH_3 (CH_3)n-$, are easily biodegraded whilst those containing a branch-chain alkyl group especially quarternary carbon atom(s) are most difficult to oxidize.

With this information, a solution was found which neither affected industry nor consumers. The branched-chain detergents were phased out and both the economy and the environment benefited. At present, with few industrial uses these so-called hard detergents are completely out of use. It is clear from this that in many cases, especially in developing countries, industries ought to be helped out of pollution problems but not condemned.

The need to protect industries and the economy in pollution control programmes has been well expressed in a lecture at Environmental Symposium in North Carolina in 1975 by Robert T. Miki, Director of Environmental Economics, US Department of Commerce. He says "Fundamental to the promulgation of national environmental regulation is a careful assessment of the potential economic impact of the specific regulation on individuals, as reflected in prices, incomes and employment; on productive units as reflected in their ability to carry on business; on the community as reflected in community income and employment; on the economy as reflected in the growth in capacity and in the ability to compete with other nations. He continues: "the consequence of erroneous actions or judgements now must be weighed against consequences in the future. If the consequence of inaccurate assessment of economic impact are to be minimized, this should be done in the formulation of environmental regulations rather than later through making adjustment after economic dislocation appears". He emphasizes, therefore, the following principles in the formulation of environmental regulations:

(a)   Careful examination of achievable technological alternative available to industry.

(b)   Pursuit of least costly way of cleaning up the environment.

(c)   Establishment of a safe minimum standard of environmental protection consonant with the objective of economic growth and stability, rather than the pursuit of an idealistic maximum standards which would involve excessive or disproportionate sacrifices by segments of the economy.

Economics certainly play a very important role in pollution control programmes. If this were not so there would be very few, if any, problems of pollution which could not be solved readily with the current state of knowledge and technology. The term "Best or Reasonably Practical" is, therefore, heavily weighted with economic implications and makes solutions to pollution problems more of cheque book rather than technical significance.

A principle enshrined in British pollution control laws, which appears to have formed the basis of pollution control in many other countries, is a useful illustration. It runs thus: "In order to safeguard industries on which the national economy depends, if even pollution is admitted by an industry, no offence is committed if the industry has taken reasonably practical means to render the effluent harmless and that such reasonably practical means are available under the circumstances of the case". However, this does not mean that industries are given a free hand to pollute. What it means is that a tremendous burden is placed on society as a whole and not industries alone to provide and maintain essential facilities for waste management. In this way, industries could be limited to basic precautionary measures that would be reasonably practical, and would not adversely affect their production and growth, but rather would allow them to discharge their primary duty to society and in the course of it operate as viable enterprises.

If we look at the British scene again, we see that the Alkaline Inspectorate (now Her Majesty's Alkaline and Clean Air Inspectorate), perhaps the oldest pollution control body in the world, established by an Act promoted by Lord Derby in 1863, started off according to Buggler (1972) as "industry's ally". In short, the inspectorate does not act as a policeman looking for a common criminal in the discharge of its duties. When an industry is faced with a pollution problem, it is first offered a partnership by the inspectorate in finding solutions. When the inspectorate is faced with an awkward and obstructive management, the practice is to advise the Trade Associations of the position. Often the recalcitrant member yields to the persuations of his fellow members. Prosecution may be resorted to only after this.

The history of the development of water pollution controls legislation in Britain also shows a great deal of accommodation for the BPT approach. The first legislation, River (Prevention of Pollution) Act 1876, was introduced with the specific aim of controlling pollution of rivers with sewage and industrial waste. Although the Act made it an offence to put solid matter and also poisonous, noxious and polluting matter into streams, there was an escape clause, based on this principle to safeguard industries. It was provided that "The Local Government Board shall not give their consent to the proceedings of a sanitary authority of any district which is the seat of a manufacturing industry, unless they are satisfied after their due enquiry that the means of rendering harmless, poisonous, noxious or polluting liquid are reasonably practical and also available under the circumstances of the case".

33

This meant that where reasonably practical means of rendering pollution harmless did not exist, polluters were free to discharge the polluting liquid into river courses.

One might be inclined to think that such a law might bring about rampant discharges of pollutants into the water courses. However, the balance is well maintained in the development processes to take care of this, for the Act also obliged the local authorities to permit manufacturers to discharge their trade waste into the authorities sewers, and under the 1937 Public Health (Drainage of Trade Premises) Act, the manufacturers were given legal right, subject to certain conditions though, to discharge their trade waste into the municipal's sewers for treatment at sewage works. (It is pertinent to note that the development of elaborate sewerage systems to take care of domestic and industrial effluents went on briskly from the beginning of the 19th century with the introduction of the water closet).

The Local Authorities also had the facility and the means to divert sewage by means of channels to convenient sites for use in irrigating agricultural lands. Provision of large-scale sewage treatment were introduced. Lime treatment, for example, was introduced in 1880 and by the beginning of the 20th century there were large numbers of sewage treatment works operating efficiently in England and Wales, and also in Scotland which operated under different, although similar, laws.

In 1951, the Rivers (Prevention of Pollution) Act was amended. This became necessary because in the Act of 1876 the terms poisonous, noxious and polluting were not defined, and their interpretations were left to the courts. This made it extremely difficult to obtain conviction under the law. The aim of the 1951 Act was, therefore, to eliminate this problem of definition. This was done by making it obligatory for industries to seek consent of River Boards before making any new/altered discharges into rivers. The discharges made into streams with the consent of River Boards were deemed not to be polluting for the purpose of the Act. However, the Boards were empowerd to impose "reasonable" conditions on the discharges as to quality, daily and hourly rates of flow, temperatures etc.

All discharges made to river courses before the 1951 Act came into force were exempted on the grounds of being fair to the old

34

industries. It was thought that these industries could not possibly comply with the minimum consent conditions that would be imposed by River Boards without investing heavily in waste management equipment and perhaps pricing themselves out of the market. However, in 1973, after perhaps giving the old industries sufficient time to readjust to changing conditions, the Water Act brought all discharges under the control of consent conditions.

It took nearly a hundred years in Britain to bring water pollution under complete control. This might be considered a long period, but it should be realized that the industrial revolution, which brought much pollution to Britain and other European countries in the 19th century, started off with the minimum awareness of environmental pollution. Industries sprang up without any restrictions on their discharges, and waste treatment was virtually unknown at the time. Because industrial growth was not planned in relation to pollution control at the time, when the need arose a delicate balance had to be struck between survival of these industries and the need to keep the environment clean.

Pollution Control Approach to Adopt

We have a lot to learn from the British experience in order to circumvent most of the problems that brought about the rather "long history". However, a useful advice has been given by Lumis (1976). He says "the gradual development of the British policy combined with physical controls of the land-use planning enables Britain to avoid the extreme measures some countries had to take to solve acute pollution problems". We may have to go by this gradual way with the existing pollution problems. However, we cannot afford to allow urban and industrial growth to take place without the necessary controls and without the provision, operation and maintenance of the supporting infrastructural services as if we are not aware of the pollution they may cause. If we did that, and there are every indications that in Ghana we are already on that path, then we may allow economic growth in terms of GNP to erode the quality of our lives and perhaps saddle our children with the tremendous burden of clearing the mess. We must, therefore, strive to achieve a balance between benefits of rising economic growth and the maintenance of environmental quality.

35

There is no justification for us to do otherwise.

We must also be careful not to adopt the technologies that have brought a great deal of pollution problems to most advanced countries in recent times. According to Professor Barry Commoner of the University of Washington, "Technologies with the slightest impacts on the environment have been driven out by ones with intense degrading impact in USA". He says "Plastics have replaced paper production. Trucks have driven out trains using five times more energy, requiring many times the land surface to operate and causing six times the environmental pollution. Shirts that were first made from cotton produced by energy from the sun are now made from synthetic fibre produced from petroleum and requiring artificial heat for production. Always the environmentally hostile product vanquished the environmentally compatible one". "Only one justification", says Commoner, "exists for this switch in technology. The new way makes more money". But one has to ask oneself why the new modes of production have proved more profitable than the old one. "The principal reason", says Commoner, "is that manufacturers employing new technology have not paid all their bills. They have treated the air and landscape as free goods. Whilst they have met such internal cost as raw materials and labour bills, they have left it to society to pay the cost of pollution" (Commoner, 1972). These are situations where traders reap considerable profits. Nations, therefore, must have clear choices as to who bears the cost of pollution abatement.

In Ghana, at present, industries pay practically nothing towards pollution abatement though part of the money which they pocket as profit ought to have gone into pollution abatement programmes. But who can blame them since no such demands have been made on them. There are several ways of obtaining such contributions from industries. These include direct taxation to raise revenue or tax incentives or economic incentives to encourage industries to invest in pollution control equipment and facilities.

Environmental pressure from various pressure groups such as "friends of the environment" could also be used to achieve improvement, and it is one of the important forces behind industrial innovation. However, where this is not applied, technological and economic benefits that may accrue to industries and the

36

country are lost.

Perhaps we have to remind ourselves that we cannot initiate another industrial revolution whose consequence will elude us until serious pollution problems are created. We can only learn from the mistakes of others and start from a broad-based approach to development; that is, development in which economic growth and the preservation of environmental quality are taken together. This could be slower in terms of per caput income, but certainly better in terms of human happiness and the preservation of the intergrity of the environment for posterity.

From what has happened so far in Ghana, it is clear that a lot of people in influential positions cannot see the tree for the forest in so far as pollution is concerned. The gradual destruction of the environment never strikes a cord so far as returns on investments are good. They argue that expenditure on pollution control constitutes investment without return and could be a major cause of inflation. Consequently, they always shy away from investing in pollution control equipment and facilities, as Royston rightly said: "investment in pollution control ... must be looked at in the same light as any other investment. Investment in new production facilities is not expected to bring financial return as soon as it is made ... (Royston, 1979)". It should also be looked upon as a form of insurance, just as no one expected one's fire insurance to pay off within the first few months or even years. But how many of us would dare to run an industrial plant without a good insurance cover.

In many developing countries, economic impact of pollution has been neglected while much attention has been paid to economic impact of pollution control. This perhaps arises from the misconception that pollution control is much more detrimental to economic progress than pollution. Although pollution has become marked in many areas, developing countries tend to delay action on pollution control due mainly to severe constraints in their economies which tend to drive all available resources into what could be perceived by them as more immediate productive ventures. But are developing countries justified in fearing that pollution control programmes will reduce economic growth? As Royston points out "Examples of Sweden and Japan may allay their fears. Sweden in 1970 when faced with economic recession deliberately introduced severe pollution control regulations linked with massive financial support in the form of grants for purchase of pollution control equipment. This stimulated construction, engineering and chemical industries and provided the motor which pulled Sweden out of the economic recession. Japan, in 1974, hard hit by the oil crisis, undertook an exactly similar policy with the result that in recent years probably 3 per cent of Japan's GNP has been rous pollution control policies anywhere in the world". Such stimulation might be due to the catalytic effect of the improved environment which enhance the image of the country, positively affects tourism and also attracts investments into industry and commerce. Royston says, therefore, that "if all countries took these examples to heart, not only would they improve the quality of their environment, but they would also stimulate their economies". In addition to this beneficial effect of pollution control, it has to be recognized that:

(1) Pollution control can never be avoided in modern developmental processes where technology and the sheer rate of exploitation defies nature's self regulatory capacities. Any feet draging, therefore, only postpones the problem and makes it more difficult to solve both technically and financially at a later time.

(2) Pollution control also creates jobs for those who work on pollution control equipment and facilities and thus contributes to the GNP.

(3) The need to keep the environment clean and in healthy condition cannot be valued in terms of present-day cost alone. Moreover, this generation like any other generation owes a duty to posterity to keep the environment in a good running order.

It is, therefore, imperative that developing countries tune their minds to the condition that pullution control should form an integral part of the development processes. This is the only way to achieve the type of growth that will satisfy the aspirations of the present and future generations.

38

Chapter 3

POLLUTION CONTROL LEGISLATION

General Considerations

Looking at the existing conditions for pollution control one wonders what sort of arrangements and legislations are appropriate to bring about effective pollution control in Ghana. We live under conditions where waste management facilities are woefully inadequate and the little that we have are improperly managed. This is the starting point from where we have to develop legislations to control pollution.

In this regard we may wish at this stage to look at the two extreme ways of pollution control from the legal point of view in order to determine the right course of action to be followed. The first is to regard pollution as a criminal offence in which case polluters are held fully responsible for infringing the law, the only alternative to complete abatement of pollution being to stop the activity that produces the pullutant. The other way is to regard pollution as a management problem in which case the cost of pollution abatement is spread wide since everybody benefits from the outcome of the development (industrial or otherwise) which brings about the pollution. Industries and other polluters could then bear what could be considered to be reasonably practical as determined by a competent authority working in close collaboration with industrialists, national economic planners, etc, and also taking into consideration the views of the general public and other interested parties. If, on the other hand, we go by the first option, many industries may have to close down since they may not afford the full cost of pollution abatement. Also, many other civilized activities such as bathing, washing and other household activities which are the major causes of pollution in developing countries may have to come to a halt. However, it may not be possible to operate solely at any one extreme. We have, therefore, to identify an appropriate course of action suitable to our environment and circumstances.

Experiences from other places have shown that some polluters may, despite the existence of elaborate facilities for waste management, sneak out at night and when nobody is likely to notice them to discharge large quantities of waste into water courses to avoid paying nominal sums for their treatment. Such polluters ought to be dealt with as common criminals. So whereas the second option might be largely preferred to form the basis for initiating pollution control legislation in Ghana and in many other developing countries, provisions should exist in our laws to deal with recalcitrant polluters.

Pollution control problems in Ghana are made worse by the lack of co-ordination among organizations whose activities affect the environment. The situation has long been recognized and although attempts have been made to bring about effective co-ordination, practically very little has been achieved. For example, the Act (Act 310 of 1965) establishing the Ghana Water and Sewerage Corporation envisaged the need for the establishment of such a co-ordinating body. Subsection 2 of Section 2 states that without prejudice to the generality of Subsection 1, the powers of the Corporation shall include: "The preparation of long-term plans in consultation with the *appropriate co-ordinating authority* established by the President". For almost a decade, no such co-ordinating body was established. Then in 1974, NRCD 239, establishing the Environmental Protection Council, gave this co-ordination powers to the Council. Section 2 (1) (b) of the Decree (*See* the Appendix) gave the Council powers to co-ordinate the activities of all bodies concerned with environmental matters and to serve as a channel of communication between those bodies and the Government.

The co-ordination envisaged under NRCD 239 requires considerable amount of data collection from organizations whose activities affect the environment for the purpose of establishing a comprehensive master plan for development. Such a master plan could then provide the basis for environmental screening of all development programmes to prevent growth that disregard the existence of supporting infrastructural facilities. Collection and analysis of data on infrastructural development will also provide the basis for investment planning and furthermore enable economic planners and decision makers to take the right decisions on

40

investment priorities. However, this function has largely been neglected.

At present, laws on pollution control and related matters are rather scanty. One of the few laws in public health is the Factories, Offices and Shops Act (328) of 1970. This law deals with health, safety and welfare of employees within the confines of factories, offices and shops. Discharge made from these premises into places outside the confines of these premises are not covered by the Act. The Act is much more of a collective bargaining tool than a public health Act. Its sole aim is to protect the health and welfare of employees and nobody else. There is the need for a much more elaborate public health Act dealing with discharges within and outside the confines of these premises to supplement other functions of this Act.

Air Pollution Control

When, for example in 1977 and again in 1981, a great deal of dust was discharged from the Tema Cement Works and from VALCO installations at the harbour into the atmosphere causing considerable nuisance and exposing the general public to health hazards, there were no laws to deal with the problem. (There are still no laws to deal with discharges into the atmosphere). As a matter of fact, it should not be too difficult to legislate against acts and omissions detrimental to health even under our present conditions. Human life and human health must always enjoy priority when weighed against the cost of pollution abatement.

Most emissions into the air directly affect human health. This is because air, unlike water, is not treated before it is ingested, except perhaps in a work environment where special devices such as masks could be worn to filter off the pollutant. Also unlike water pollution control problems, air pollution control problems do not require elaborate infrastructure to deal with them. Individual industries are normally responsible for the provision of the necessary facilities for the abatement of air pollution. This makes the "polluter pays" approach more applicable to air pollution control than to water pollution control.

In most air pollution problems, the use of obsolete equipment and the lack of proper maintenance of machinery have been the

41

main causes of excessive emissions. Some industries also take advantage of the legislative vacuum not to install the appropriate equipment. Controlling authorities may, therefore, need to introduce and enforce strict guidelines to ensure good house-keeping at work places. Since "add-on" pollution abatement facilities cost more and are much more difficult to install technically, there is the need for the controlling authority to ensure that, at the planning and the development stages, industries adopt the "best practical technology" to prevent the emission of noxious and offensive gases into the atmosphere. A very high level of success in air pollution control can be achieved at a very low cost if control measures are applied at these stages.

The application of the "best practical technology" to old industries may, however, have to be tempered with much leniency since many of these industries may find difficulties, both technically and financially, in installing the acceptable pollution abatement equipment. For example, when it was found in the UK that for the effective dispersal of pollutants from brick-making factories into the atmosphere, chimney stacks should top 91.44m, it was discovered that older brick kilns could not take the weight of the taller stacks and the brick companies also wanted many more years of service out of their old faithful kilns.

The way to establish what constitutes the "best practical technology", in the case of old industries, is to strike a balance between the technical possibility of getting a pollutant removed on the one hand and the cost on the other in order to determine the type of equipment, if any, to be installed to abate pollution. A technical possibility would be considered impracticable if the cost is so high that the operation of the industry would be rendered unprofitable or nearly so. Care must, however, be taken to prevent "the best practical technology" from being interpreted as the "cheapest practical technology". If this happens, industries may not be under any obligation to provide acceptable solutions to air pollution problems. This situation places considerable burden on the controlling authority to do its home work well in order to ascertain exactly when a technical possibility is not economically feasible so as to prevent industries and traders from taking undue advantage of the pragmatic nature of the law.

In the absence of any legislation on air pollution control in

Ghana, some industries do, however, take precautions to ensure that waste discharged into the air is not unduly dangerous. For example, VALCO has a chimney which tops 152.40m (Fig.9) sufficiently high to dispense poisonous fluorine compounds into a large volume of air for greater dilution to reduce their effect on the ground. Cattle and livestock which eat grass contaminated with fluorine compounds may suffer from fluorosis, a kind of bovine version of rheumatoid arthritis which involves additional bone damage and dental decay. Evidence shows that the amount of fluorides occurring in grass around the area where livestocks are kept is below 22μg/g (Danso, 1986). This amount is below the threshold concentration.

Water Pollution Control

The control of water pollution on the other hand could be exceedingly complex (*See also* Chapter 6). This is mainly because, unlike air pollution control, water pollution control requires the commitment of a substantial amount of public funds into the construction, operation and maintenance of sewer, sewage treatment plants and other waste water management facilities and equipment without which water pollution control laws would be largely unenforceable. But many decision makers in developing countries do not see their way clear to do this mainly because it is not easy to justify this heavy investment on any factor which could be seen to be very pressing especially in a depressed economic situation. For example, it is not easy to establish correlation between the occurrence of diseases and water pollution. Decision makers see, therefore, no real justification for such huge investment.

If water pollution is looked at from a broader perspective, however, it is realized that it affects the legitimate uses of these waters in several ways. For example, when sewage effluents are discharged into water courses, they enrich these water bodies with plant nutrients which encourage eutrophication and silting up of lakes (*See* Chapter 6). In man-made lakes in which huge investments have been made such siltation is clearly undesirable especially if it is realized that the state of eutrophy is irreversible. Water pollution also affects fisheries (Mackenthun *et al* , 1945) and where there is excessive growth of aquatic weeds it may affect fishing

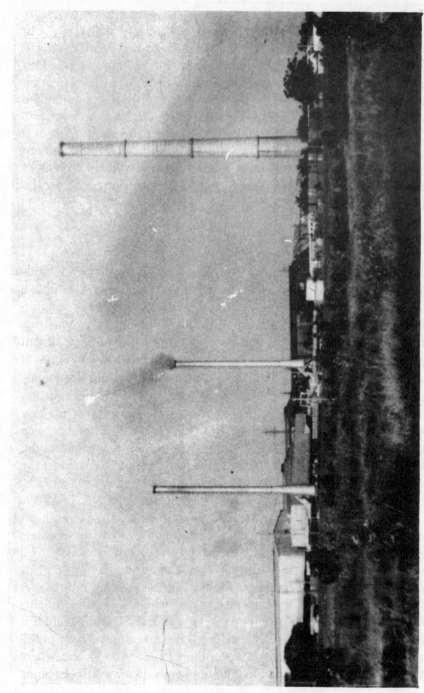

Fig.9. The VALCO plant at Tema. (Fluoride compounds are discharged

and navigation. Excessive growth of weeds in rivers and water channels also cause flooding and the destruction of property. Water pollution also affects the scenic value of water bodies and thus affects recreation and amenity uses of these waters and, therefore, has negative effect on tourism. It is, therefore, much better to look at the totality of the problems caused by water pollution including damage posed directly or indirectly to human health in order to create the right atmosphere for effective control. In order to convince decision makers of the need for it, we have to make accurate assessment of all the damage it may cause to society and to the environment. It must be admitted, however, that it is not easy to place values on such factors as human health and happiness or even on tourism but somehow this must be done.

Flowing directly from the attempt to avoid this heavy investment is the general feeling in Ghana that in water pollution control programme, it is possible to pass the buck to the polluters. Thus, emphasis is laid much more on enactment of legislation than on the provision and maintenance of facilities for waste water management. This certainly places the cart before the horse and makes these laws largely unenforceable.

Legislation exists in Ghana to protect natural waters and public sewers (LI 1233, Ghana Water and Sewerage Regulations 1979 Sections 11 and 12). Yet, sewers which are supposed to be protected under the law and the facilities for treating wastes to make them fit for discharge into natural waters, are woefully inadequate and the little that exist are poorly maintained. As at 6th June, 1986, the only sewerage system under the control of the Ghana Water and Sewerage Corporation was the Contract S/1 system in Central Accra. This system which cost a great deal of money in foreign exchange is heavily under-utilized because large portions of the area covered by the system have sub-standard housing and chaotic arrangement of houses and plumbing in most parts of the area will never meet the standard for connection to the system until complete urban renewal is carried out in the area. There is also the problem of the high cost of connecting to the system and the inadequacy of water supply to cater for such high level of service. Meanwhile, waste water from houses, factories, etc., in the country including the area covered by the system are discharged into drains and gutters not under the control of the Ghana Water and Sewerage Corporation, but city, urban and district councils which take very little responsibility for waste water management. The waste from these drains then empty into rivers and other bodies. How could natural waters be protected under such circumstances? Under the existing laws neither the district councils nor the Ghana Water and Sewerage Corporation take full responsibility for waste water management. It is quite obvious then that there is the need for a separate sewerage authority to be completely in charge of waste water management. Although the law assigns substantial responsibility to the Ghana Water and Sewerage Corperation for the management of waste water, since its establishment in 1965, the Corporation has been bugged down by the problems of water supply to the extent that waste water mangement has been a forgotten child.

Under the Ghana Water and Sewerage Regulations 1979 (LI 1233) Section 1, it is stated that the Corporation may by a notice published in the *Local Government Bulletin* declare any area specified in the bulletin to be a connection area. Also under Section 1(3) "The Corporation may, in consultation with Town Planning Authority, establish planned connection area for any area where water and sewerage connections exist before development," and under Section 2(1) "where an area is declared a connection area . . . the Corporation may take over the operation of any private sewerage system existing in the area". Since the introduction of this legislation, no area has been declared a connection area and no private sewerage system has been taken over, although a large number of them in very poor state do exist in Accra and other places.

Again, in the case of the protection of natural waters, Section II of LI 1233 says "no person shall throw, empty or turn or suffer or permit to be thrown or emptied or to pass into any natural water courses:

(a) Any matter that may pollute the water. . . .

(b) Any chemical, refuse or waste steam or any liquid of a temperature higher than forty-five degree Celcius. . . .

(c) Any industrial effluent unless upon conditions prescribed by the Corporation and upon express permission by the Corporation to do so".

As usual, the Corporation has shown very little interest in the implementation of this law. Even so, the enforcement of the law will be too difficult, since there are no reasonably practical means of waste treatment and disposal other than to dispose of such untreated wastes into water courses.

The LI 1233 has some semblance to the British water pollution laws especially the Rivers (Prevention of Pollution) Act 1951 of England and Wales. But at the time this legislation was introduced in England and Wales, there were elaborate and well-maintained sewerage systems and sewage treatment plants in that country under the control of public health authorities. River Boards, which were in charge of river pollution control at that time were, therefore, in a position to enforce the law to achieve approximately the desired aim. If the effluents do not meet the standards for discharge into rivers, industries had the option to discharge them into public sewers for treatment at sewage works. These sewage treatment plants like the Mogden Sewage Works at West Middlesex, England (where the author had his industrial training) have been in continuous and efficient operation for many years. In Ghana, there are a few scattered sewerage systems and sewage treatment plants, none of which is operating or being maintained in accordance with the designer's intentions. Worst still, none of these plants deal with industrial wastes (*See* Chapter 1, Sanitation).

Industries and other dischargers of pollutants in Ghana, unlike in Britain, do not have any reasonably practical alternative for the discharge of pollutants other than to discharge them into water courses. The question might be asked, why shouldn't polluters especially industries, be made to render their effluents completely harmless before discharging them into water courses. There are several reasons why this would be unfair and impracticable in many instances.

(1) In most developing countries, the bulk of pollution load comes from domestic sources rather than from industrial sources. The cost of pollution abatement should, therefor, be borne much more by the whole community rather than by industries.

(2) Most industries cannot afford the cost of full sewage treatment on site and much so because their initial plans do not envisage future incorporation of sewage treatment

47

facilities.

(3) Most industrial wastes are difficult to treat alone unless mixed with domestic waste.

(4) The smaller sewage treatment plants put up by industries may not enjoy the advantage of lower running cost associated with large works.

(5) Since the construction, operation and maintenance of sewage treatment plants consume a lot of money and do not contribute to profit, they could easily get neglected by management. When that happens, there will be a large number of small malfunctioning sewage treatment plants sited all over the place which could be eye sores, constituting serious health hazards and creating their own pollution problems.

An example may help to illustrate some of these points. There are two breweries in Accra: the Accra Brewery Ltd and the Achimota Brewery Ltd. The Accra Brewery Ltd discharges its effluents into the Contract S/1 sewerage system while the Achimota Brewery Ltd discharges its effluents into the Odaw stream which empties into the Korle Lagoon. Brewery effluents are made up, largely, of carbohydrates and they suffer from nutrient imbalance. Such effluents do not provide good substrate for the biological oxidation process in the treatment of sewage. Even where large quantities of brewery effluents are discharged into an existing biological sewage treatment plant they upset the treatment process, causing sludge "bulking" in the activated sludge plants and excessive film growth and "ponding" in the biological filter plants. For brewery effluents to be treated alone, therefore, costly physico-chemical process may have to be adopted. But in Accra where the Odaw Stream and the Korle Lagoon are grossly polluted from domestic sources alone, what should be the justification for asking the breweries and for that matter other industries to undertake such costly assignment? The most appropriate solution would be the provision of a community sewerage system and sewage works into which individual industries would discharge and pay some amount towards the treatment and or disposal perhaps after some pretreatment.

One would like, at this stage, to caution against attempts to copy environmental legislation from developed countries. Britain,

48

for example, was for a long time a world leader, and her systems and institutions took a very long time to evolve and are very complicated. Legislation supporting these complex systems and institutions are also complex and scattered. For example, if you copied British water pollution control legislation, the straightforward sanctions against offenders may not reveal anything to you about complementary provisions in public health which give relief to these sanctions. You may, therefore, end up having a piece of unworkable legislation.

At an International Conference on Global Water Law Systems held in Valencia, Spain 1 – 6 September, 1975, the following observation was made among others. "Most legal systems discussed in detail were drawn from the developed world. There seems to be a tendency to take these legal systems as models to be superimposed on developing countries with only minor modifications. Problem of technology transfer, lack of adequate infrastructure and differing socio-economic and cultural conditions will make such process not very useful. One should start with a knowledge of local conditions and devise a system to suit them".

Most often it is necessary to set up a powerful committee comprising of people knowledgeable in waste management and in pollution control as well as planners, decision makers, and other interested persons to study the problems and establish the basis for the introduction of appropriate legislation. The following suggestions are put forward as providing some guidelines for tackling the problem in Ghana.

(1) Attempt should be made to invest in the provision, operation and maintenance of infrastructural facilities and to allow infrastructural development to direct and control growth. Appropriate legislation should be enacted to give effect to this.

(2) Planning and urban management regulations should be updated and strictly enforced.

(3) A separate authority should be appointed to hold consultancy for all aspects of waste management and to prepare the grounds for investment in waste management facilities.

(4) Legislation should be introduced to raise revenue from industries and other dischargers of pollutants in aid of (1) above. Economic incentive approach could also be used

49

to raise revenue. In this regard, a charge could be levied on the volume and pollution load of effluents discharged into the environment by industries and other dischargers of pollutants. Apart from raising revenue, this will serve as economic disincentive for them to continue to pollute and will force them to adjust to the most practical solution available, including recycling of waste, replacement of obsolete equipment, maintenance of plant and equipment to bring efficient use of raw materials in order to reduce pollution load and waste treatment where practicable. This system can be used to direct development and also as a measure for siting industries (that is if the charge is related to the assimilative capacity of the receiving media at various sites, traders would be directed to sites where it is less costly to discharge pollutants).

(5) Facilities which already exist or should have been installed for the abatement of pollution should be inspected and appropriate legislations introduced to enforce their installation, operation and maintenance in accordance with designer's intentions.

The above suggestions are necessary to prepare the ground for the introduction of strong measures. For in pollution control, the establishment, operation and maintenace of facilities for waste management are necessary prerequisite for the introduction of strong measures. At some stage, the two can grow together and provide evidence to the fact that economic growth and pollution control could be partners in progress.

Previously, the practice in water pollution control has been to proscribe by law the discharge of poisonous, noxious and polluting substances into water courses (e.g. Section II(a) of LI 1233). However, the difficulties arising out of how to define poisonous, noxious and polluting led to the problems of enforcement and little success was achieved. Another approach has been to define these parameters in law by stating definite standards for the discharge of effluents in the law (e.g. Section II(b) of LI 1233). Although this approach makes legal proceedings less cumbersome, it has several problems associated with it. It does not take into consideration the conditions in the receiving water course such as dilution provided and the intended use of the water course. These factors may make the standards more or less, restrictive in many instances. Changing of such standards when the need arises may also be laborious since they are written into law, and can be changed only through the due process of the law.

A more recent approach has been to request, by law, all dischargers of pollutants to seek the consent of the controlling authority before making any discharges (e.g. Section II(c) LI 1233). In granting their consent, the authority is empowered to impose reasonable conditions, normally conditions achievable under the best practical technology approach, taking into consideration local factors such as dilution provided and the intended use of the receiving water course.

Legislation allowing such flexibility can be operated successfully in a society where there is a disciplined approach to development and where waste management facilities are provided and maintained at sufficiently high level. If this happens not to be the case, any minimum conditions imposed by the controlling authority would be difficult to achieve practically. Consider the breweries example cited above. Here the only reasonable option available to the Achimota Brewery under the present circumstances is to do nothing about the effluents until there is an opportunity to discharge into a community sewerage system.

In the advanced countries, the practice in the past has been to exercise greater restrictions on the discharges into inland waters than into estuaries and coastal waters. This has resulted in some estuaries and coastal waters becoming grossly polluted. Most of these countries are now saddled with the problem of how to clear the mess. At present, restrictions originally applied only to inland waters in these countries have been extended to estuaries and coastal waters.

In Ghana, at the moment, there is a proposal that the discharge of raw sewage into the sea through an outfall is "the correct ultimate solution" (*See* Chapter 1). This perhaps will set us on the same trail as that of the advanced countries. Apart from the fact that construction of sea outfall involves sophisticated technology and is very expensive, it has to be noted that the sea water does not sterilize sewage (Buckley, 1974). For example, concentration

51

of 40,000 coliforms per 100 ml had been measured in Forth Estuary in the United Kingdom at distance of 1 km from the discharge point. Again it has been noted that when sewage is discharged into salt water it rises to the surface forming sewage slick which could spread over greater distance and more often than not are washed to the beaches where they cause health and aesthetic problems. A way to minimize these problems may either be to construct longer outfalls or to provide some treatment to allow for the construction of shorter outfalls.

The provision of full sewage treatment before discharging into the sea may definitely cost higher but we need not dismiss it outright because of the cost. In some cases, this may have to be weighed against the benefits likely to accrue from the use of the beaches for recreational and other purposes before a decision is taken.

Chapter 4

TOXIC CHEMICALS ADMINISTRATION

Risk Assessment

Toxic chemicals have been in use in many developing countries for agricultural and public health purposes for several decades now. However, in most of these countries, there are no monitoring systems in operation to assess their effects on humans and other biota and there are also no control meausres to regulate their importation, distribution and use. This situation has given rise to considerable amount of uncertainty concerning the hazards these chemicals pose in the various environments and has created room for over-reaction on the one hand and under-reaction on the other hand to the use of these chemicals. This situation is unfortunate and is due to an ever-increasing demand for these chemicals in these countries to control pests which wreak considerable havoc in agriculture and in public health. As far as we can perceive at the moment, it is not possible to feed and maintain the health of the ever-increasing populations in these countries without the use of these chemicals. It is, therefore, incumbent upon us to establish and maintain efficient monitoring and control systems for the judicious use of these chemicals

Nearly all of these chemicals have some disadvantages connected with the obvious benefits accruing from their use. Although we can easily criticize many of these substances in this way, it must always be remembered that man consciously exploits a chemical in the constructive belief that on the balance it will be of real use to society. Even the most dangerous chemicals are deliberately produced as ultimately beneficial; that is only so long as the benefits of use are generally thought to outweigh the cost will a particular chemical remain on the market. The clear recognition of all known benefits, cost and likely risks involved in the use of the chemicals and the assessment of their balance point are, therefore, central to the control and management of these chemicals in any society.

Normally before a chemical is released into the field, comprehensive testing procedures are employed by industry to ensure that it has no serious disadvantages under its designated uses. However, on some occasions with certain drugs or pesticides, harmful or inconvenient side-effects have emerged during production, usage or disposal. Such inadvertent or unexpected side effects may so alter the balance of cost and benefit that a chemical may no longer be regarded as appropriate for its purpose, and its usage has to be restricted or it has to be withdrawn.

Most of our knowledge of the effects of these chemicals are derived from acute toxicological and medical studies. But since environmental effects are generally associated with chronic exposures, studies must also be made on the long-term continuous exposures to minute amounts of these chemicals in the environment. Most often, aquatic wild life and resources appear most sensitive with man apparently the least affected. For example, a million times the amount of DDT that will kill trout in 100 days is found in a healthy US worker formulating DDT for 20 years (Table 6). If, therefore, we base our control measures on the effect on man alone, we may miss altogether very serious environmental effects which may eventually have serious adverse effects on man. The assessment of the effects of these substances must, therefore, always include the long-term chronic studies on wild life. However, risk assessment in general must involve the following:

(1) Toxicological studies: This is the study of the effects of the toxic chemicals on humans and on other biota. It is normally conducted under controlled conditions and involves (a) short-term (acute) studies, and (b) long-term (chronic) studies.

(2) Assessment of levels: This involves the determination of residuals of the chemicals in air, water, soil and biota. This indicates the exposure levels of these chemicals and provide the basis for epidemiologic studies.

(3) Epidemiologic assessment: Epidemiology describes the circumstances under which disease occurs within and between population groups. It can be used to discover an association between exposure to a chemical and the occurrence of disease.

54

TABLE 6

Range of Levels and Effects of ΣDDT^+ in the Biosphere (Expressed as ng/g Fresh Material to the Nearest Factor of 10)

0.01	in sea water, blocked development of certain calanoid copepods
0.1	in rain falling over the UK and cerain oceans
1	untreated soils in remote areas
1	solubility of p.p[1] DDT in water
1	in water, may kill some trout in 100 days
1	average daily intake/g body mass, from UK human diet
10	WHO/FAO proposed acceptable daily intake for man/g body mass
10	fresh cow's milk in the UK
100	in fat of Weddal seal and penquins, Antartica
100	in fresh human milk (UK and US)
1000	in human fat UK
1000	in US late trout fry high mortality at late yolk-sac stage
10,000	in human fat (US)
10,000	in fatty tissues of grey seal (SW England) and common seal (E and NW Scotland)
10,000–	experimentally lethal concentration in brains
100,000	of many birds and animal species
100,000	in diet, experimentally induced significant eggshell thinning in mallard but not in coturnix quail
1,000,000	in fat of healthy herring-gull ǂ slightly impaired reproduction
1,000,000	in fat of healthy adult phesants ǂ with chick survival 90% of normal
1,000,000	in fat of healthy US worker formulating DDT for ca 20 years
10,000,000	in pectoral muscle of white-tailed eagle found dead (Stockholm Archipelago)

Notes on Table 6

    (1)   Data abstracted from numerous scientific papers in current literature

    (2)   All organisms were alive and apparently healthy and unaffected unless otherwise stated

+   DDT = DDT + DDD

‡   Some mortality in adult populations

Source: Goodman, G. T. 1974.

Risk Regulation

After considering risk assessment, we must now consider how risk is regulated and how the law must seek to define the minimum safe levels of exposure to toxicants. As discussed earlier, this does not depend on risk assessment alone but on complete cost benefit analysis in which risk, certainly, is an important factor. Since the results of cost benefit analysis might differ from country to country, it is possible that a chemical might be banned in one country but might still be in use in another. Also, a chemical might be carcinogenic but if the expected life-time risk is below a certain level it might still remain in use. In other words, it is held that the law must deal with unreasonable risk. For example, animal studies on saccharin, a food sweetener, led the US Food and Drug Administration (FDA) to announce in March, 1977 that it intended to ban the sweetener because it was carcinogenic. However, faced with strong public pressure, and evidence from a group for whom saccharin was medically recommended, the US Congress passed a law in November that same year, prohibiting FDA from taking action. It was found that the dosage of saccharin fed to the rats in the study were far in excess of what a human would consume under the designated uses. It was like drinking 1250 x 340g diet beverages a day over a life time, that was 532 l of liquid or over 4000 packets of saccharin a day for a life time. For obvious ethical reasons much toxicological work has to rest on extrapolations to humans of investigations carried on test animals. But since man is not a big rat some extrapolation may have limited validity. In recent times, the Codex Alimentarius Commission (CAC), a

56

joint creation of FAO and WHO, has been trying to establish internationally-acceptable food standards. The CAC has been defining levels of pesticide residues acceptable in food. The maximum levels have been based on "the practical certainty that injury will not result after a life time of exposure".

There are situations where no risk at all can be tolerated under the law. This is normally associated with very dangerous chemicals like nuclear waste. In certain cases, comparative risk or risk-to-risk approach is adopted. Here the health risk of not using the substance is compared with the risk of using it. This was applied in a decision to use chloroform (Ricci, 1985), a potential carcinogen, to kill bacteria in drinking water. This approach is used mostly in the approval of new prescription drugs, but it is seldom used in the environment area.

With pesticides and substances not directly consumed by man, a balancing approach is normally adopted. Under this approach, a substance may be banned if it poses an unreasonable risk of injury or illness. This approach weighs or balances a health risk such as the per cent rise in the incidence of the disease against economic benefits, jobs and other intangibles. It must be admitted that it is not easy to assign values to most of these factors, but the important thing to note is that a chemical is not banned simply because it has been found to cause some form of illness. If this were to be the case, no chemical would remain on the market. Even under certain conditions (normally under emergency conditions), a banned chemical may be allowed for use. For example, in the US, Section 18 of the Federal Insecticide, Fungicide and Rodenticide Act allows exemptions of this kind under emergency conditions. The term "emergency conditions" has been defined as an unusual set of circumstances calling for non-conventional use of pesticides. One example would be a heavy infestation of insects that would result in substantial reduction in the expected farm yields and profits (e.g. the locust invasion of the Sahelian region in Africa in 1986). Another example would be a loss in value of fixed assets such as land, brought about by pest emergency.

Some amount of risk is always encountered with almost all human activities and the use of toxic chemicals is quite prominent among such activities. However, with judicious application of these chemicals based on knowledge and sound management principles, a country always reaps considerable benefits from these chemicals. What is required then is a considerable amount of work in the areas of risk assessment and cost benefit analysis to provide the necessary data for management, for good information is always the best basis for the sensible administration of any problem.

In the UK, two schemes have been established to control the use of pesticides throughout the country. These are the Pesticides Safety Precaution Scheme (PSPS) and the Agricultural Chemical Approved Scheme (ACAS). PSPS is responsible for all aspects of safety with regard to the use of pesticide including giving approval for and monitoring the use of pesticides in the country. ACAS is responsible for certifying that a chemical does what the manufacturer claims it does (efficacy), before approval is given for its use.

In Ghana, The Environmental Protection Council is responsible for the safety aspects with the use of these chemicals. It has a toxic chemicals committee and has so far succeeded in compiling a list of pesticides in use in the country, indicating their known side effects. The Ministry of Agriculture, through its various organs, has also been responsible for ascertaining the efficacy of these chemicals. However, a co-ordinated effort with legislative backing to control and manage these chemicals in the country is lacking. One would, therefore, like to offer suggestions in this direction for the control of these chemicals in the country.

Guidelines for Toxic Chemicals Control

Based on the principle that the law must deal with "unreasonable risk", the following are offered as some guidelines for drafting legislations for toxic chemicals administration in countries where these laws do not exist. This model is suggested with the problems of Ghana in mind.

(1) Manufacturers and importers must be required under the law to register all the toxic chemicals they deal with within a specified period. Such registration should be renewable at given regular intervals.

(2) A levy may be charged for the registration and a licence issued.

58

(3) All toxic chemicals already in manufacture in the country must qualify for automatic registration.

(4) All toxic chemicals imported which have continuously been brought into the country for some period (to be determined) before the coming into force of the regulations must also qualify for automatic registration.

(5) For all other toxic chemicals, a permit should be obtained before action commences for their manufacture or importation.

(6) Application for permit should provide the following information among others.

    (a) The intended use(s) of the chemical.

    (b) Whether or not the chemical is to be manufactured under licence.

    (c) A sample of the chemicals to be manufactured under licence or to be imported should be submitted with the application.

    (d) A report from the manufacturer specifying the following:

        (i) The efficacy of the chemical

        (ii) The composition of the chemical

        (iii) The designated uses

        (iv) All known hazards

        (v) Whether it is banned in the country of origin and if so for what reasons.

(7) Guidelines or procedures for determining the acceptability or otherwise of the chemical must be spelt out by the law. This should include guidelines for packaging, labelling and handling.

(8) Application for permit should not be unreasonably withheld (period to be specified).

(9) After the expiry of the period, if nothing has been heard from the controlling authority, permit should be deemed to have been granted.

(10) Permit or licence already granted can be withdrawn or the use of the chemical restricted if the chemical proves later on to pose unreasonable risk of injury or illness or to have unreasonably affected fauna and/or flora, and also export and other interests.

(11) Notice for the withdrawal of permit should be published for a minimum period (period to be specified) before permit or licence is withdrawn.

(12) Reasons for the withdrawal of the permit or licence should be spelt out clearly in the notice.

(13) Any aggrieved person(s) should have the right to appeal against the intended withdrawal within the notification period.

(14) Provision should be made for exemption in the use of chemical especially under emergency conditions.

(15) Precautions should be taken under such emergency conditions to prevent the chemical(s) from posing unreasonable risk.

These guidelines provide the general framework within which legislations could be prepared for the control of toxic chemicals in the developing countries. In many of these countries, sentiments run very high against the use of pesticides and other toxic chemicals, especially with the reports that these chemicals are being dumped in these countries by the rich industrialized world. There is certainly a genuine fear that multinationals are cashing in on the inability of many developing countries to monitor and exercise controls. But if developing countries recognize the role these chemicals are playing in solving world food problems (UN 1974) and also improving the health of their people, they would rather not panic but heed the advice contained in UNIDO publication (UN 1983) that "developing countries must be mindful of the need for information and training to exploit the new technology in the most socially cost-effective way. This is the way to avoid over-reaction as well as under-reaction both of which do not serve the interest of the people in developing countries.

Chapter 5

STANDARDS SETTING AND POLLUTION MONITORING

Standards Setting

Pollution control legislation goes with standards or guidelines for effluents discharged into the environment. The basis for setting such standards could be many and varied depending on what one is aiming at. Some people advocate uniform standards for pollution control whilst others want flexibility in standards setting based on the intended use of whatever mediun is receiving the effluents, the dilution it provides and also the effect directly or indirectly on public health either alone or in combination with other substances already existing in the environment. Another factor is whether pollution is likely to have international consequences or not, and if so there might be the need to adopt certain rigid international standards.

In Europe, for example, most rivers are international rivers and therefore certain stringent uniform standards are necessary to control river pollution. Otherwise, countries in the lower reaches of the river may suffer from relaxed standards of upstream users. Britain, since she joined the European Economic Community (EEC), has been under considerable pressure to adopt the community's uniform emission standards. She has, however, opposed the adoption of such standards, because British rivers unlike European ones are generally fast flowing and could, therefore, take more pollution load since turbulence of fast rivers brings about better re-aeration for better oxidative breakdown of organic matter. Moreover, Britain is an island and British rivers flow only in Britain. But EEC argues that relaxed standards in Britain could make British products cheaper on European markets where industries are expected to spend more money to achieve high quality effluents. But this argument, according to Britian, overlooks the principle of "comparative advantage" which is particularly fundamental to the operation of the common market. According to this principle, the welfare of all concerned is maximized if countries specialize in producing those goods which they can produce relatively cheaply than other countries and then trade with other countries, exchanging these relatively cheaply-produced goods for imports from the other countries which would have cost relatively more to produce at home". Another argument which is particularly worth noting is that, "application of uniform emission standards would provide incentive for continuing to locate industries in worst site from environmental point of view. It would mean that all should behave in a manner appropriate to the most disadvantaged and it would imply that all industry should incur the same labour cost per unit of output as those of the least efficient firm".

As a contrast to having uniform emission standards, ambient standards allow for the use of stream capacities, for example, for waste treatment purposes, and it makes it possible to avoid undue restriction where, the quality of the river, the dilution it provides as well as its intended use may not justify such restrictions. Though it is not possible to see very far into the future on this, flexibility in standards setting appears much more appropriate in developing countries bearing in mind the need to introduce stricter measures as and when they become necessary.

As a hypothetical case, suppose a paper mill company wishes to establish a factory on the Densu River downstream of the dam at Weija. According to the company, they will require 9.1×10^6 l of water a day for production. Effluents from the factory will contain mainly fibres, fillers such as china clay, adhessive agents and dyestuff, etc. The company plans to provide sedimentation as the only treatment. And the resultant biochemical oxygen demand (BOD), according to the company, would be about 60 mg/l. Statistical data on the Densu River show that during the dry season there is virtually no flow of water downstream of the dam from the lake, a situation which is bad from the ecological point of view. This means that the factory's effluents will be the only water in the river bed downstream of the dam during the dry season and with the BOD of 60 mg/l this section of river would go septic with offensive and objectionable odour during this period.

If the same factory was sited near the Volta River at say Akuse, there might not be any need for pretreatment before discharging the effluents into the Volta River which could provide more than

2000 times dilution at the minimum discharge rate. Assuming the dillution to be 2000 times, and the BOD of the river and of the pre-treated effluents to be 2 mg/1 and 60 mg/1 respectively, the resultant BOD would be about 2.03 mg/1 and there would be no significant change in the quality of the river. If the untreated effluents with BOD of say 200 mg/1 is discharged into the Volta, the resultant BOD will be about 2.1 mg/1 and that will still not produce any significant effect. So whereas the factory might even be allowed to discharge its effluents untreated into the Volta without any adverse effect, complete waste treatment might still create problems at a site downstream of the Weija Dam.

For the purpose of standards setting, a look at the substances discharged into the environment reveals that there are two types of waste products which are causes of pollution (Goodman, 1974). These are:

(1) Those which involve either an increase in volume or rate of introduction of substances which are already present in the environment (Protochemicals).

(2) Those products such as poisons and chemicals including atomic waste which are not normally present in natural ecosystem (Allochemicals).

In the first type, protochemicals, we are dealing with organic waste such as sewage and ordinary minerals which are present in low concentrations in all ecosystems. Setting standards for these products is not very difficult since biological means of controlling their amounts can be applied. Here the environmentalist is concerned chiefly with imposing restrictions on flow rate, volume, concentrations, temperature, etc., so that the natural biological processes would be sufficient in the receiving media to control them.

However, it is the second group of pollutants, allochemicals, which pose great problem because of the difficulty of setting standards for them. A large number of these substances, agricultural chemicals, insecticides etc., are introduced into the field every year some of which are toxic below levels at which they are chemically detectable and also little is known about the chronic toxicity of most of them. Most of our knowledge of the effects are derived from acute toxicological studies on man, but data from several

63

scientific publications show that aquatic wildlife or resource species appear to be most sensitive, with man apparently least affected (Table 6). Also different groups of scientific specialists concerned solely with human health or with resource species or with aquatic or avian organisms have sometimes assumed that the safety levels peculiar to their own interest apply universally. In the past, this may have led to some medical authorities being dismissive or complacent about potential risks to biota and to some biologists being alarmists about potential risk to man. This has frequently confused attempts to make rational appraisals of the cost and benefits in the use of DDT, and similarly for several other chemicals. Since most of these chemicals are very popular in Ghana for agricultural and public health uses, it is very essential that we take the study of the effects of these substances on resource species and on man seriously in order to introduce the appropriate restrictions on their uses at the right time. This is not an easy task because of the difficulty of recognizing such effects when they occur in the field. In the field, factors such as hunger, disease, overpopulation, predation, competition, availability of oxygen etc., have effects similar to the effects on the toxic substances. There is also the problems of the effect of weather and the synergistic effect of certain substances. For example, sulphur dioxide is more damaging to the human being in the humid climate than in the arid climate. Arsenic and zinc also exhibit synergistic effect, their combined toxicity being significantly higher. All these factors make standards setting extremely difficult for these substances.

Standards setting also has legal implications: (a) should standards be made statutory in which case the standards are defined by law and could be altered only by law, or (b) should they be made non-statutory in which case the law does not say anything about the specific standards. These are left in the hands of the controlling authority. Here there is a presumption that if industries meet certain minimum standards prescribed by the authorities it means that they are employing the best practical means to avoid pollution. This does not mean that the standards must be set in an aribitrary fashion. They must be worked out between the controlling authority, industries and national economic planners, based on achievable technological alternatives available to industry and other dischargers of pollutants, in relation to the prevailing conditions. These standards can always be altered to take account of improved technology. These two alternatives have their merits and demerits for whereas statutory standards could make legal procedures less cumbersome, they are quite laborious to alter when the need arises. Non-statutory standards are, however, very difficult to enforce since there is a large element of subjectivity inherent in the approach to the setting of such standards.

However, in a developing economy one would like to favour pragmatism in pollution control. It appears, therefore, that basing standards on conditions under which discharges are to be made (i.e. making use of ambient instead of uniform emission standards) and also making standards non-statutory are better options. We are beginners and may, therefore, need to change standards more often. The most important consideration, however, is to ensure that there are well-trained and competent personnel to be in charge of pollution control.

A great deal of baseline studies are required in the process of standards setting. There is for example, the need to know the conditions in which the rivers and other water bodies are, especially the natural conditions of the water bodies unaffected by man, in order to follow the trends in deterioration or otherwise of these water bodies, and provide appropriate standards at the appropriate time. Most often, standards have been based only on chemical parameters but in recent times biological parameters have become prominent. Biological investigation can show the effect of intermittent discharges of poisonous substances which the chemist may miss all together. The biologist can also easily pinpoint the source of the trouble by moving up to the point where the biological effect begins. The chemist can do this only if pollution is continuous. However, biology has largely been neglected because it is apparently not a quantitative science. But this situation is being looked at seriously with the introduction of biological indices based on various types of quantitative assessments. If it is considered that pollution is basically a biological phenomenon in that its primary effect is on living things, then one may wish to encourage more use of biological parameters.

Pollution Monitoring

For legal as well as managerial reasons, it is considered more appropriate to commission a single body to undertake the legal monitoring. Research Institutions and Universities may undertake monitoring but they may not be allowed into certain areas for the following reasons:

(1) The first reason is that the trade secret acts forbid the disclosure of analytical results. Analysts working on trade effluents may have to take an oath to keep the results secret. Not many people consider this as very important these days because it is contended that if one is looking for the manufacturing process going on in a factory in modern times the last place one would look for it is from the effluents.

(2) Secondly, in prosecution, the courts are not likely to accept analytical results from any organization which has no statutory function to undertake such an assignment since such an organization cannot be under any obligation to conduct the test with judicious precision.

(3) The third reason is based on what the controlling authority wants to do with the results. There might be a situation where although there is an infringement, the medium receiving the effluent and or the treatment thereafter is such that no damage is caused to health or to the environment. The authorities may, therefore, wish to overlook such an infringement. This ought to be kept secret from other polluters who may complain of unfair treatment and perhaps fight for more relaxed standards. Bodies with no legal or managerial responsibility cannot be trusted to hold such information secret.

There is of course no fool-proof measure against leakage of such information but one ought to be making serious attempts to provide the basis for sound managerial process.

Standards setting which should be a continuous process should not be limited to the discharge of effluents alone. It should provide modalities and guidelines for all development processes including the design, construction, operation and maintenance of waste treatment plants and facilities. This ensures that their

66

operational efficiencies are in consonance with what is expected from such facilities. In this way, it is easier to introduce enforceable legislation and to ensure free co-operation between economy, science and government in the area of pollution control.

Chapter 6

POLLUTION CONTROL IN FRESH WATER BODIES

Introduction

Fresh water bodies require special attention in pollution control programmes due to their important role in waste management. Almost all pollutants no matter where they originate eventually end up in water bodies either through rains from atmospheric sources or as leachates from underground or surface dumping sites. This makes water pollution control an important function especially because water is one of the basic essentials of life. It could even be argued that all life is aquatic since water is both essential and the most abundant substance in the protoplasm. However, we normally speak of an aquatic habitat as one in which water is mainly an external as well as internal medium.

Water occupies about three quarters of the earth's surface. Fresh water habitats, however, occupy a relatively small portion as compared to marine and terrestrial habitats, but their importance to man is far greater than their area due to the following reasons:

(1) Fresh water bodies are the most convenient and cheapest source of water for domestic and industrial uses.

(2) Fresh water components are the limiting factors in the hydrological cycle.

(3) Fresh water bodies provide the most convenient and cheapest waste disposal systems.

These factors emphasize the need for efficient management of fresh water resources so as to ensure that they do not become a limiting factor for man, of course bearing in mind that one can neither run industry nor sanitation without producing effluents that must be discharged somewhere. And as Klein (1957) remarked, "water pollution like crime, disease and road accidents will eventually be brought under control but will never completely be eliminated".

Pollution adversely affects the legitimate uses of fresh water bodies in diverse ways. Some of these uses are, water supply, irrigation, navigation, fisheries and fishing, recreation and amenity. It is important to state here that the legitimate uses also include the use of these water bodies for waste disposal. If this is appreciated, then waste water management would be seen in its right perspective and one would have a clear view of the balanced interests in the use of fresh water systems. For as long as the water body is capable of assimilating these substances, this could be a legitimate and sensible use of resources. Although all the uses mentioned above are essential for the happiness and well being of man, with urbanization and industrialization it may be too difficult to maintain all these uses on all fresh water systems. Some of these systems, for example, may have to be given up largely to effluent disposal. In any case, some of them in their natural state, unaffected by man, may not satisfy the requirements for all these uses.

Of the legitimate uses mentioned above perhaps the one which appears to be most difficult to justify, in Ghana at the moment for pollution control purposes, is the recreational uses of these waters. Our depressed economic situation has tended to place emphasis on more mundane values such as improving the basic standard of living than on recreation. Some other factors which also account for the general lack of interest in the recreational uses of fresh water in the country are that none of the big cities and urban centres are sited on any important rivers and also most tropical rivers carry considerable amount of sediments due to the nature of tropical rainfall which causes considerable erosion. Aesthetically, therefore, many of these rivers do not look any different from polluted waters especially during rainy season (Fig.10). In the developed countries on the other hand where almost everybody enjoys treated pipe-borne water, investment in water pollution control has been based largely on the grounds of recreation and wild life conservation. It is, however, hoped that with the emphasis being placed on tourism at the moment recreational uses of these waters may become more important in the near future and perhaps attract the desired investments.

Investment in water pollution control in a developing economy on the other hand could more justifiably be based on grounds of public health and eutrophication with its various adverse effects

Fig.10. Densu river looking very turbid after series of heavy rains. (Picture by Dan Offei).

on fisheries and fishing, navigation, flooding, siltation of lakes, etc.

Public Health

Pollution control in relation to water supply and public health in general is quite a complex issue especially under the environmental conditions of most developing countries. Theoretically, it is the treatability of the pollutant and not the mere presence of it that affects the potability of water. However, in a country like Ghana where many people drink untreated surface water, the problem assumes different dimensions. And it will be quite natural for people to think that under such circumstances stringent measures are required to control water pollution. However, it should be appreciated that it would be too difficult, if not impossible, to maintain potable water quality in surface waters. This would be impracticable in many instances due firstly, to the habits of the people, including rampant defaecation, washing and bathing in these waters. Secondly, it is not a reasonably practical proposition to consider rendering waste waters completely innocuous before discharging them into surface waters. And thirdly, most surface waters unaffected by man do not meet drinking water standards. What appears to be reasonable is to accept the present situation where many people rely on untreated surface water as the only source of drinking water as the base from where we aim at providing treated pipe-borne water for everybody. It will definitely take some time to achieve this, but such a decision would prevent us from taking panicky measures that would not solve any problems. Public health education may help to some extent in improving the quality of surface water and in protecting drinking water sources, but a decision like this is unavoidable in the natural consequence of utilizing the assimilative capacities of these water bodies for waste treatment purposes. One, of course, has to be very careful with this where there is great variations in the discharge rate of the stream. Dilution is very important in the use of stream capacities for waste treatment purposes; therefore, the minimum discharge rate as well as the duration it takes are very crucial in deciding how much waste to allow into a particular river (Table 7).

In pollution control, it is the worst possible conditions, not the average conditions, as well as the rate of occurrence and the dura-

71

TABLE 7

Discharges and Sediment Load of Some Coastal Rivers in Ghana

River	Discharge (m^3/Min)		Max/Min Sediment Load(mg/L)		
	Max	Min	Discharge Max Ratio	Max	Min
Alabo River at Pore	29.45	0.17	173	659.0	207.0
Ankroba River at Dominase	439.0	95	4.6	534.0	225.0
Ayesu River at Ochreko	65.14	0.34	192	604.0	255.0
Pra River at Beposo	1764	260	68	450.0	253.0
Tordzie River at Tordzinu	29.03	0.93	31.2	1590.0	251.0
Nakwa River at Ekotsi	51.26	0.37	138.5	587.0	264.0
Ochi-Amissa River at Mankesim	82.2	1.1	74.2	1290.0	194.0
Densu River at Manhia	106/1	0/8	132.5	658	12

Source: Ayibontele, Nii Boi and Tufuor-Darko, T. 1979. *Sediment Loads in the Southern Rivers of Ghana.* Accra: WRRU, CSIR.

tion of those conditions, which are important. Worst conditions such as low flow rate of the river, high temperatures which increase rate of biological oxidation and heavy pollution load can within a short period render a river or a portion of it completely lifeless, highly objectionable and absolutely unsuitable for other purposes. Such conditions might also create irreversible problems. The oft quoted example is someone with his head in the oven and feet in the freezer. The average temperature of his body might still be normal but he will certainly neither be alive nor could ever be. However, aquatic life cannot be treated in the same way as human life in pollution control programmes, for unlike human beings who have identifiable personalities, it is not the life of any particular aquatic organism that we wish to protect. It is aquatic life in general which may always reappear when conditions return to normal. Consequently, where pollution does not directly affect human life, it is proper, for effective management, in order to keep cost as low as possible and to maintain a balance of interest in the use of such rivers, to interprete such occurrences statistic-cally. For it might be much more desirable to permit some of these occurrences if the duration is short and the interval between them long enough, than to prevent them altogether.

Allochemicals

In the use of assimilative capacities of fresh water bodies, great care must be taken where the inclusion of toxic and non-biodegradable wastes is unavoidable. Toxic chemicals can within a short period render a river completely lifeless and pose danger to public health, whilst non-biodegradable waste may accumulate through food web to dangerous levels in top canivores and pose similar danger to public health. A considerable amount of experi-mental work has been done on the effect of these toxic substances on fishes in order to find out what concentration could be allowed in rivers. This work has been reviewed by several authors (Hynes, 1974).

If it is considered that fish and other aquatic organisms are exposed continuously to waters containing these toxic substances, then it becomes clear that in water pollution control, fish life, in a way, takes precedence over human life, since this exposure makes lesser concentrations of toxic substances much more inju-rious to fish than to human. For this reason, factors based on fisheries and aquatic wild life requirements (rather than on public health requirements) provide better safeguard for the maintenance of good water quality (Table 6).

Fish is a very useful indicator of the real state of purity of water (Turing, 1947). No river should be considered as in a satis-factory condition unless fish will live and thrive in it. Furthermore, there are lower animals, e.g. *Daphnia magna,* which are much more sensitive to toxic subtances than fish (Redeke, 1927; Ellis, 1937) and, therefore, could be used as indicator organism in place of fish where higher quality of water is required.

In the discharge of toxic substances into fresh water systems the idea of threshold dose as it is applied to therapeutic drugs in human context is not very useful (Wuhrman and Woker, 1958). Instead, we speak of threshold concentrations, for a creature which is exposed continuously to low concentrations of toxic substances is in a different predicament from the one which receives a single dose. In the determination of threshold concentrations, the important thing is whether the particular poison is metabolically destroyed in the body or not. For those poisons which are destroyed metabolically it is legitimate to speak of tolerable concentrations. For other poisons such as heavy metals, there is theoretically no concentration at which they are harmless. They merely become less harmful at greater dilution (Hynes, 1974). It is, therefore, important that where toxic substances are used in the environment, an efficient monitoring system is maintained to assess continuously the effect of these substances on resource species and on man for the effective control of the use of these substances in the environment. Where it is not possible to exclude toxic and non-biodegradable substances from discharges, stringent standards ought to be set for these substances bearing in mind not only their concentrations but also their synergistic effects.

Protochemicals

With substances normally present in natural ecosystems such as organic wastes, the important thing is to control the concentration and the rate of discharge of such substances so that the natural processes would be sufficient in the receiving water courses to deal with them. One could make use of an indicator organism for the maintenance of the required water quality in this regard, but the organism need not necessarily be the most sensitive depending upon the intended use of the water and also the socio-economic value of the organisms in that particular water. With organic wastes, standard based solely on a certain minimum dissolved oxygen levels provides sufficient assurance for the maintenance of certain minimum water quality levels. Factors to be considered here are:

   (i)   Maximum discharge rates of the effluents
   (ii) Minimum discharge rate of the river
   (iii) Maximum temperature attained by the river
   (iv) Turbulence
   (v) Depth of the river
   (vi) Presence of oils and detergents.

Reasons for making use of worst possible conditions such as maximum discharge rate of effluents, minimum discharge rate of the river and maximum temperature have been discussed earlier. Turbulence and depth of river give indication of the aeration capacity in the river as well as distribution of oxygen throughout the water body. Turbulent shallow rivers might be well oxygenated throughout the whole water body whilst deep sluggish rivers may contain less dissolved oxygen especially in the deeper layers. Oils and detergents can form protective film on the water surface and hinder reoxygenation.

The discharge of organic wastes into water bodies brings about uptake of dissolved oxygen in the oxidative breakdown of these wastes. A certain minimum dissolved oxygen level is attained in the river depending on the factors discussed. As the river flows downstream, organic matter is reduced and the comsumption of oxygen is also reduced. Aeration causes the oxygen level to rise again and the general characteristics of the water may revert to the original condition (Fig.11).

In the event of discharge of heavy pollution load, however, very low dissolved oxygen concentration may be obtained and putrefaction may set in. A carpet of sewage fungus may appear and the anaerobic breakdown of organic matter may produce obnoxious odours. Deoxygenation also produces its own toxic effect through the production of toxic substances such as hydrogen sulphide and ammonia from the anaerobic digestion of organic matter. But where highly nitrified effluents are also discharged into these polluted waters, nitrates provide oxygen for bacterial breakdown of organic matter in preference to sulphates and phosphates. This may help to alleviate the problem of the release of these obnoxious and toxic substances. This could be practised where treated and highly nitrified effluents are to be discharged into tidal waters and the lower reaches of rivers not needed for water supply purposes and where eutrophication problems are not likely to crop up or are of minimum importance.

Where low dissolved oxygen levels are experienced, the discharge of organic waste may also have indirect effect on public health by disturbing the ecology of the river or water body and thus encouraging the abundant development of nuisance and disease-causing organisms. Most aquatic organisms cannot survive where concentration of organic matter is high enough to produce total deoxygenation. Under such circumstances, the normal river fauna may

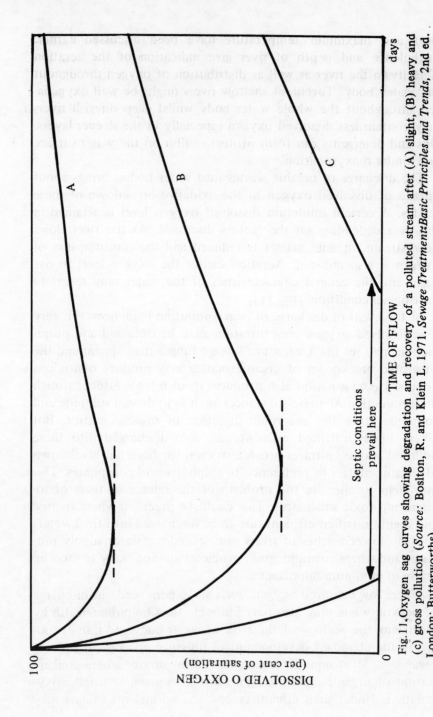

Fig.11,Oxygen sag curves showing degradation and recovery of a polluted stream after (A) slight, (B) heavy and (c) gross pollution (*Source:* Boslton, R. and Klein L. 1971. *Sewage Treatment:Basic Principles and Trends,* 2nd ed. London: Butterworths).

be replaced by the larvae of nuisance and disease-causing organisms such as the mosquito (*Culex pipiens*), the mothfly (*Psychoda* sp.) and the bee-fly (*Eristalis* sp.). These larvae have structures that enable them to take in atmospheric oxygen. They have air tubes at the tip of their tails which they keep at the surface of the water whilst the rest of the body is immersed in deoxygenated water rich in organic matter. Their normal habitats are water, rich in organic matter and so often deoxygenated. The best-known way to keep populations of these organisms low is to improve the quality of these water bodies and thus increase the dissolved oxygen contents for the survival of the normal aquatic fauna to maintain the ecological balance.

Eutrophication

When dealing with water pollution control in the tropics, one very important consideration is the discharge of plant nutrients into aquatic ecosystems. Organic waste, whether treated or untreated contains a great deal of plant nutrients and when these are available in aquatic systems, they may cause excessive growth of weeds and phytoplankton. The result of this process is normally what is described as eutrophication. With tremendous amount of sunshine all year round and the sluggishness of rivers, eutrophication could be a very serious problem. This certainly enjoins us to be careful with utilizing stream capacities for waste treatment purposes in the tropics.

Also, the building of dams to create man-made lakes have always resulted in ecological changes that tend to create conditions favourable for eutrophication. Eutrophication is particularly detrimental to man-made lakes due to the rapid siltation that it tends to bring about in these lakes (the aquatic weeds die and accumulate in the lakes). Eutrophication might also affect fisheries, fishing and nagivation. There are reports of deaths of fishes caused by the decay of algal blooms (Mackenthun *et al.*, 1945).

A river or a stream might contain a great deal of plant nutrients. The turbulent nature of the flowing water might, however, prevent the development of algae and aquatic plants. When such a river is dammed, the quiescent lacustrine environment suddenly becomes conducive to the growth of weeds provided other conditions are favourable. One such condition of great importance, and with its roots in pollution, is the availability of limiting plant nutrients

77

mostly nitrates and phosphates. Of the two, nitrates are much more easily available in water courses than phosphate because:

(a) nitrates are more soluble in water than phosphates and even where the two are liberally applied in fertilizers, phosphates become strongly bound to soil and do not easily find their way into water courses (Thomas, 1970);

(b) certain algae, the blue green algae, can fix nitrates from atmospheric nitrogen.

Consequently, where phosphates are freely available in water bodies, it is very probable that effluents resulting from certain human activities mostly domestic and industrial activities, might be responsible. Apart from the amount that is normally released, from the oxidation of organic matter in sewage effluent, one major source of phosphates is from the use of detergents at home and in industry.

In all newly-formed lakes, there are two main sources of nutrients for the growth of aquatic weeds:

(a) Nutrients already present in the river before it is dammed.

(b) The newly-flooded area always contains a great deal of organic matter which decay and release large amounts of plant nutrients.

The second source contribute a great deal to eutrophication in all newly-formed lakes and the duration of the state of eutrophy in such lakes depends on several factors including:

(a) the rate at which nutrients are replenished from outside (inflows), and

(b) the rate of recycling of nutrients in the lake.

Where these two factors do not contribute significantly to nutrient budget of the lake, the initial outburst of algae and plant growth subsides after a few years and the lake stabilizes. However, lakes have the ability to add to their own nutrient status by trapping and recycling nutrients (Berg et al., 1958).

This is the basic reason why eutrophication tends to be a continuous and irreversible ageing process in many instances. The trapping of nutrients has been observed in some Lake District lakes of England (Pearsall et al., 1946). Table 8 gives the average amount of saline nitrogen in water entering and leaving these lakes. From these data, it was estimated that Windermere gained about eight tonnes of nitrogen in this way during the year, and

78

this when built up into plankton, represents a dry weight of about 100 tonnes of organic matter. When these weeds die, they decay and their nutrient salts are released and if conditions are favourable they become available together with fresh inflows for the increased growth of weeds. In this way, the lake becomes increasingly more eutrophic. Perhaps the best way of controlling eutrophication is, therefore, the physical removal of these weeds from the environs of the lake. This represents nutrient loss to the system and gradually bring about reduction in nutrient load. The destruction of weeds, either through the use of herbicides or by employing herbivores to graze down the weeds does not represent nutrient loss to the system, and where conditions are favourable for the circulation of nutrients, that might even bring about increased eutrophication. Moreover the use of herbicides may affect the abstracted use of water for potable supply and for irrigation (Brooker and Edwards, 1973).

TABLE 8

Average Amount of Saline Nitrogen in Inflow and Outflow Water of Some Lake District Lakes of England

Lake	Inflow Water	Outflow Water
Thirlmere	0.51	0.53
Windermere	0.71	0.55
Esthwaite	1.16	0.74
Lowes Water	0.02	0.35

Sources: Pearsall, W. H., Gardiner, A. C. and Greenshilds, F. 1946. Fresh water biology and water supply Britain. *Scientific Publication. Fresh Water Biology Association* 11, 90pp.

The problem of eutrophication became manifest on two man-made lakes in Ghana: Weija Lake (closed in 1975) and Barekese Lake (closed in 1969). The Weija Dam was constructed on the

79

lower reaches of the Densu River, and there are two large urban centres, Nsawam and Koforidua, upstream from where untreated wastes are discharged into the Densu River. There are also some villages and a great deal of farming activities upstream of the Barekese Lake on the Offin River.

In the initial stages of formation of these lakes, there was profuse growth of aquatic weeds (Fig. 12). However, in recent times, the growth of the weeds seems to have subsided on the Weija Lake. The growth of weeds, however, rages on the Barekese Lake. Nutrient released from decayed organic matter definitely contributed immensely to the initial outburst, but it is difficult to say whether the Weija Lake is stabilizing now as explained above, or whether successive lower rainfall in recent years in the area (Table 9) and some other not-too-apparent factors might have suppressed the growth of weeds. Successive lower rainfall with reduced turbulent inflows might allow for the locking up of plant nutrient at the bottom mud. This, aided by lack of strong winds, could prevent circulation of plant nutrients. (There are many other contributory factors the discussion of which is beyond the scope of this book). If this is true, then the problem is likely to be on the increase again when higher rainfall with consequent turbulent inflow, such as storm waters, stirs up the bottom mud and causes circulation of plant nutrients.

Another factor which might have contributed to the reduction in weed growth or cover is the lower rate of flow of water in the river beds due again to lower rainfall. This allows for the removal of plant nutrients by both rooted and floating aquatic weeds in the riverine section. Evidence of this could be seen clearly at Nsawam bridge upstream of the Weija Dam where one can hardly see the water in the river bed due to weed cover. When the floods come, these floating aquatic weeds might be pushed into the lakes together with considerable amount of mud, rich in plant nutrients, from the river beds. With the problem of eutrophication in mind, there is the need to look far into the future with the aim of mapping out the intended uses of these rivers before utilizing their assimilative capacities for waste-treatment purpose. In any case, it would be very interesting to know to what extent these lakes have silted up since the closure of the dams and the rate at which this is occurring. These data are needed at least to inspire efficient

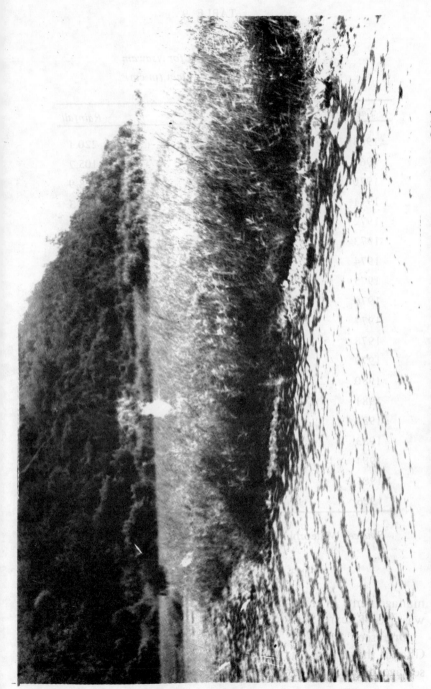

Fig.12. Profuse growth of weeds on Weija Lake. Picture taken in 1980. (*Picture by Dan Offei*).

81

TABLE 9

Annual Rainfall Data for Nsawam
Upstream the Weija Dam (in cm)

Year	Rainfall
1968	220.1
1969	105.7
1970	128.9
1971	118.3
1972	122.9
1973	118.3
1974	142.3
1975	96.4
1976	95.9
1977	93.8
1978	101.5
1979	163.9
1980	144.9
1981	122.4
1982	116.0
1983	64.6
1984	137.7
1985	106.2
1986	98.3

Source: Meteorological Services Department.

management of man-made lakes in the future and to prevent wastage of scarce resources.

One sees from the seriousness of eutrophication problems in Ghana that there is the need to practise nutrient removal in sewage treatment processes especially in the inland cities and urban centres. In the case of non-point source discharges mainly from agricultural lands, it might be necessary to limit farming activities in the catchment area of the water to be protected. However, with regard to point source discharges, plant nutrients could be removed before such effluents are discharged into water course. It is economically desirable to utilize the nutrients for one form of production or another since their discharge into water courses is an appalling waste of resources added to the pollution they cause. Nutrient in purified sewage could be removed by spraying it onto land (Imhoff, 1955), the fertility of which would then be increased by absorption into the soil or by holding the sewage in shallow ponds where algae would be encouraged to grow and could be removed together with their nutrient salts. Such ponds could also be utilized in economically-feasible projects for fish production especially in the tropics where there is plenty of sunshine for algal growth.

In Calcutta, India, where raw sewage is fed into fish farms, productivity exceeding 900 kg/ha-year have been achieved. However, it is possible to achieve higher productivity than this in the tropics with the *Tilapia* especially *Sarotheroden*. Yields as high as 2500-3000 kg/ha-year with ponds fertilized with sewage effluents has been achieved (McGarry, 1978).

Technology is also well advanced for the use of sewage and solid waste for the production of biogas. Such plants are in use in several countries in Asia. It is estimated that there are over 10,000 plants in operation in India; 29,000 in Korea; 7,000 in Taiwan and 80,000 in China (MacGarry, 1978).

In Ghana at the moment, the scale of water pollution problems is no where near what obtains in the industrialized world. However, some serious problems exist in lagoons and streams draining the big urban centres. The trend in deterioration is also clearly discernible, and it is desirable that plans are initiated now to utilize the large amount of resources going down the drains to the economic benefit of the country as is being done elsewhere.

Causes Of Water Pollution

Water pollution problems in Ghana could be attributed to three main causes:

(1) Urbanization and industrialization,
(2) Agriculture,
(3) Water resources exploitation.

Urbanization and industrialization

Urbanization and industrialization, as discussed in Chapter 1, pose a very serious problem to water bodies since almost all waste from municipal and industrial sources eventually arrive in these water bodies. Pollution especially water pollution, therefore, becomes more serious as population densities increase and as urbanization and industrialization become more intense. However, discharges from these sources, unlike those from agricultural sources, are point-source discharges which with proper planning and management could be dealt with to get pollution load reduced to tolerable limits.

Looking at the chaotic situation which characterizes urban growth in Ghana one wonders how much filth from these sources arrive in the water bodies and what are the capacities of these water bodies to deal with the filth. At present, there is not much information on these. However, judging from the sluggishness of rivers in the country, the lower dissolved oxygen contents of tropical waters and the higher rate of oxidative breakdown of organic matter due to higher tropical temperatures, one wonders how much organic load could be allowed into these bodies without impairing their other legitimate uses. Already some rivers carry considerable amount of organic load from leaf-fall and detritus material. To arrest further deterioration in the qualities of rivers in the country, planners and decision makers ought to give priority attention to waste management. The idea that investment in pollution control constitutes investment without return ought to be discarded, because the improved image and the higher quality of life a country derives from such investment is known to have stimulated economic growth in many countries.

One major hindrance to investment in pollution control in many developing countries is the lack of environmental policy directives in the development process. This is due partly to lack of proper institutional arrangements, partly to lack of "know how" and partly to lack of strong environmental lobby. The depressed economic situation in most developing countries tends to de-emphasize these factors, but certainly this is the time to stimulate action in these areas so that the prevailing survival instincts which have tended to place emphasis on more mundane values do not force us to cut our noses to spite our faces.

One outcome of lack of policy in the area of pollution control in Ghana is that industries pay nothing towards pollution abatement. This creates a misconception especially among up and coming industrialists, who have no knowledge of what happens elsewhere, that they can damage the environment at no cost to themselves, whereas a reasonable percentage of the money they pocket as profit should have gone into pollution abatement programmes. In order to prevent such a misconception from gaining roots, government ought at this time to introduce appropriate legislations and policies to guide people to behave in a manner consonant with sound environmental development. For example, the policy of charging industries according to the volume and pollution load of effluents they discharge into the environment is known to force these industries to adopt the most practical solution available to them in order to reduce such charges. Such actions, which include recycling of waste, maintenance of plant and equipment to bring about efficient use of resources, waste treatment where practicable, always bring about improved environment and also efficient use of natural resources.

There are several rich industries in Ghana which pollute inland waters and make them unfit for several purposes beneficial to the people without incurring any liabilities. For example, diamond mining companies at Akwatia, Kade and Edubiase discharged mine wastes containing considerable amounts of suspended solids, mostly silt, about 18,000 mg/1, into the Birim River (Mensah, 1976). The resultant turbidity of the river downstream of the mines could be as high as 800 NTU; see Table 10). The ecology of the river might be greatly affected (Pentelow, 1949; Larsen and Olsen, 1950; and Paul, 1952) and this also makes it too costly to use the river downstream of the mines for potable water supply. Akim Oda, a large urban centre downstream of the mines with a population of about 25,000 people has, therefore, to depend on unreliable borehole supply of water.

Most of these industries which pollute inland waters (see examples in Table 11) are in a position to provide some form of treat-

TABLE 10

Water Quality of River Birim at Selected Stations

River/Station Date	PH	Turbidity (NTU)	Total Hardness (CaCo₃)	Colour (Hazen Units)	Dissolved Oxygen	Chloride	Iron	Calcium	Magnesium	Free Carbon Dioxide
(Before Discharge)										
Birim/Kade										
24.8.60	9.3	14.0	39.2	40	—	6.0	0.16	—	—	—
29.9.60	6.9	53.0	26.6	160	—	5.0	0.94	—	—	—
22.11.61	6.9	59.0	25.7	225	—	4.0	0.80	—	—	—
27.8.64	7.1	44.0	27.0	78	—	4.0	1.30	—	—	—
18.12.64	6.9	70.0	28.0	95	—	6.0	1.60	—	—	—
11.11.65	7.5	—	25.0	95	—	7.0	1.50	—	—	—
10.12.65	6.3	—	29.0	95	—	6.0	1.20	—	—	—
13.7.66	7.1	—	29.0	95	—	6.0	0.70	—	—	—
13.8.70	7.1	25.2	35.0	50	7.8	8.0	—	5.6	5.2	28.0
Birim/Bunso 1.2.73	7.5	—	74.0	10	—	22.0	—	15.2	9.7	9.7
Supong/Nsutam 1.2.73	—	27.0	25.0	15	—	14.0	—	4.0	3.6	29.0
(After Discharge)										
26.5.60	9.3	370.0	35.3	320	—	6.0	0.0	—	—	—
Birim/Akim Oda 29.10.61	7.1	332.0	30.4	650	—	6.0	0.22	—	—	—
27.8.64	7.1	700.0	32.0	450	—	4.0	1.10	—	—	—
11.11.65	6.9	—	27.0	180	—	7.0	2.00	—	—	—
19.10.66	6.9	—	25.0	225	—	10.0	2.80	—	—	—
13.8.70	6.9	878	33.0	750	7.1	10.0	—	4.8	5.2	5.2

Notice Turbidity of the river after discharge of mine waste (Diamond mine washings) at Akim Oda, Kade and Bunso are upstream the discharge points

Source: Mensah, Gertrude G. 1976. *Water Quality and Pollution Survey of Inland and Coastal Water of Ghana.* Accra, WRRU, CSIR.

TABLE 11

Some Industries and Effluents Discharged into Inland Waters

Industry	Product	Effluent Volume ($10^6 l$/month)	Composition	River into which effluent discharged
Ghana Consolidated Diamond Akwatia	Diamond	202.93	Suspended solids mostly silt approximately 17,790 mg; very turbid.	Birim
Cayco Kade	Alluvial Diamond	2.75	Suspended solids, silt; very turbid	Birim
Ghana Consolidated Diamond Ltd. Edubiase-Oda	Diamond	35.35	Suspended solids, silt; very turbid	Birim
State Gold Mining Corporation Konongo	Gold Bullion	81.83	Cyanide, arsenic silt, iron, gold	Owere
Prestea Gold Mines	Gold Bullion	95.5	Cyanide, arsenic, silt, iron, copper, zinc, gold	Ankobra
Tarkwa Gold Mines	Gold Bullion	25.00	Cyanide, arsenic, silt, iron, copper, zinc, gold	Ankobra
Ghana National Manganese Corporation	Manganese Ore	283.67	Fine clay and laterite traces of oil	Ankobra
Ghana Rubber Estate Bonsa Tyre	Natural Rubber Tyre	6.96	Dirt, serum from latex, carbon black	Bonsa
Ashanti Goldfields Corporation	Gold and Silver Bullion	100.0	Cyanide, arsenic, silt copper, gold	Offin
GIHOC Nsawam	Alchoholic Drinks Canned Fruits and Vegetables	1.66	Organic waste	Densu

Source: Adapted from Mensah, Gertrude G. 1976. *Water Quality and Pollution Survey of Inland and Coastal Waters of Ghana.* Accra: WRRU, CSIR.

87

ment if the law so demands. Some of these industries are in isolated places and do not have the advantage of getting their effluents discharged into municipal sewers, where this is available and also practicable. There is, therefore, no alternative but to get these industries to provide for waste treatment and disposal where this is necessary and practicable.

There are some industries which although are sited in urban centres may still have to undertake some form of pretreatment before their effluents are admitted into municipal sewers. Such effluents may carry heavy sediment loads which may block sewers, contain toxic chemicals which may be injurious to biological oxidation of sewage or may contain strong acids and alkalis that may affect the fabric of the sewers.

In the siting of industries, it is necessary to take into consideration the type of effluent to be discharged. With toxic waste containing substances, e.g. heavy metals, which are difficult to remove beyond certain limits, it might be necessary to have such an industry sited where heavy dilution with other waste is possible to reduce the effect on biological sewage treatment. Depending on the dilution, it is possible to treat such toxic wastes at sewage treatment works employing the normal biological oxidation process. The treatability of such toxic chemical wastes has been worked out (Bolton and Klein, 1971). The 5-day Biochemical Demand (BOD) of crude sewage is normally 3—5 times the 4 hour Permanganate Value (PV). Toxic industrial wastes can give a ratio as low as 0.2. Industrial sewage containing inhibitory trade wastes may give BOD/PV ratio intermediate between 0.2 and 3.0 depending on the proportion of trade waste present (Table 12). Bolton and Klein (1971) suggested, therefore, that the BOD/PV ratio may be regarded as giving a general indication of the relative ease with which substances present can be oxidized biologically. In practice, the discharge of industrial wastes could be regulated to achieve the desired mixture for treatment by the normal biological oxidation process.

Where the discharge of such wastes to treatment works may create problems, it might be necessary to discharge them directly into rivers depending on the dilution provided and also the intended use of such rivers. In the discharge of heavy metals into aquatic systems, one has to bear in mind that these metals get

precipitated and concentrated in the bottom mud. Certain organisms, e.g., oysters, cockles, mussels and clams which feed by
means of syphonic devices from the bottom can, therefore, concentrate these metals in their bodies to dangerous levels. One,
therefore, has to take into consideration the dietary and economic
importance of these organisms in that particular river or water
body before making discharges containing heavy metals into
waters containing such organisms. If need be, it might be necessary
to employ costly physio-chemical methods to render such effluents
highly innocuous before they are discharged into such waters.

Agriculture

Agriculture (non-point source discharge) affects aquatic sytems
in several ways. In the first place, clearing the land increases surface run-offs and loss of water into the underground water resources. It also increases incidence of flooding and destruction of
property. The incidence of leaching of plant nutrients into water
bodies is increased. This problem is made worse in the tropics by
the torrential nature of rainfall and also the increased use of che-

TABLE 12

Typical BOD/PV Ratio for Some Waste Waters

Waste Water	5–Day BOD 4–Hour PV	Biological Oxidation
Birmingham Domestic Sewage	4.0	Easy
Birmingham Industrial Sewage	1.8	Rather Difficult
Toxic Chemical Waste	0.2	Very Difficult
Dairy Wastes	9.0 – 3.0	Very Easy
Farm Wastes	2.0 – 3.0	More Difficult Than Sewage
Slaughter House Waste	7.0 – 11.0	Very Easy

Source: **Bolton, R. and Klein, L. 1971.** *Sewage Treatment: Basic Principles
and Trends,* 2nd ed. London: Butherworths.

89

mical fertilizers. The leaching of plant nutrients from agricultural lands contributes immensely to eutrophication and, unlike point-source discharges from municipal sources, they are extremely difficult to control unless farming activities in the whole catchment area of water to be protected are curtailed.

Pesticides that are used in agriculture (as well as those used in public health) may eventually arrive in water bodies and might cause fish diseases and fish kills. They might also promote eutrophication by eliminating zooplankton and other herbivores that feed on phytoplankton. Pesticides that are persistent in the environment can also be delivered by the normal biogeochemical cycle to an unknown sensitive species including man; so ideally all chemical substances used in the environment should be either passive or if active, have a half-life in the environment of less than a week (Goodman, 1974). Thus, organophosphorus pesticides although extremely toxic, oral LD 50 3 to 6 mg/kg for parathion (Ben-Dyke, Sanderson and Noakes, 1970) may never move far from their site of application, being destroyed in a few days. Relatively speaking, they do not constitute an environmental hazard.

Water Resources Exploitation

It is not only the discharge of pollutants into water courses that impairs the legitimate uses of these waters. Exploitation of these water resources for various purposes also have tremendous adverse effects on these waters and on the environment in general. Two of such exploitation of significance in Ghana are:

    (a) Construction of dams to create man-made lakes.

    (b) Utilization of underground waters.

Dams. The construction of dams to create man-made lakes have several useful purposes. Some of the primary uses are water conservation and water storage for domestic and industrial uses, provision of hydroelectric power, flood control to protect people in the lower courses of the river, irrigation, fish farming, commercial fishing, navigation, leisure and recreation. However, man-made lakes have several problems associated with them e.g., resettlement, diseases, movement of materials of archaeological value, inundation of natural resources, and secondary salination.

90

Resettlement. The problem of resettling people displaced by the floods is always a major one. When for example the Volta Lake, the largest man-made lake in the world (8,500 km^2) was formed, about 80,000 people in 739 villages comprising more than 1 per cent of the population of Ghana had to be resettled. A preparatory Commission Report recommended cash compensation but this was rejected due mainly to the experience from the Damodar Valley Project in India where 91 per cent of the people to be resettled chose cash compensation in preference to accepting land for land and house for house. The result was mass migration into Indian cities and later effort to recolonize the people from the streets of the cities onto farmlands had little success (Jopp, 1965). Further reasons for the rejection was the large number of people involved and the lack of time to mobilize them in self help projects.

The villagers were, therefore, encouraged to participate in Government resettlement schemes. Those who did not wish to do so were given cash compensation. In all, 69,249 people in 12,799 households chose to be resettled while 9,036 people in 1,858 households chose to resettle themselves.

Under the Government resettlement scheme, "core" or "nuclear" houses were to be provided. Under this scheme only one room was to be constructed before settlers moved in. The rest of the house was to be constructed by the settlers. Even so most of the "core" houses were not completed due to the fact that vigorous planning restrictions created bureaucratic constraints. When the settlers moved into these uncompleted "core" houses, the cost of obtaining items like cement and bitumen was prohibitive in terms of family income.

The completed "nuclear" house was also too small and this was compounded by the fact that most families were polygamous with the wives requiring separate rooms. There was overcrowding and the average number of people per room was 2.2 compared to 1.4 in the flooded villages. This happened despite the fact that total population in the villages was down to 43,500 because of migration (FAO/UNDP, 1971). These conditions forced many young girls and boys onto the streets in the cities.

Diseases: With the change from riverine to lacustrine environment, many diseases may become prevalent around newly-formed lakes. Some of these diseases which are known to occur in tropical areas are Onchocerciasis and Schistosomiasis.

Onchocerciasis or river blindness is a disease of the fast-flowing rivers, and dam constructed could have a negative effect on it except in areas around spillways where the vector *Simulium damnosum* could become prevalent. The snail vector of schistosomiasis, however, becomes much more prevalent in the newly-created quiescent lacustrine environment.

In order to prevent the diseases, it may be necessary to have settlements sited away from infected shores of these impoundments and to provide them with their own water supply. This siting applies both to irrigation channels and man-made lakes. However, where fishing is a major occupation, it may be unrealistic to have these settlements sited far away from the lake. Under such circumstances, alternative measures might have to be taken to control the disease.

In irrigation practices, the overhead sprinkler without run-off is considered safest for tropical countries to prevent schistosomiasis. But health consideration can hardly dominate decision between the overhead sprinkler and the canal. The latter can be fenced near settlement or pipe where this is possible. In canal construction, lining and flow rate are crucial as smooth surface is less attractive to snails and rapid flow dislodges them. In Japan, concrete lining has been used to reduce snail numbers and water seepage at the same time. Canal maintenance can also reduce snail population, for vegetation harbours snails and lowers water velocity.

Total prevention of the diseases is, however, not possible. But with thorough study of each situation, it is possible to reduce the disease problems considerably and at reasonable cost.

Movement of monuments: This problem was especially encountered in the Nile Valley during the construction of the Aswan Dam where there were many ancient monuments that had to be moved. Despite the effort and the amount spent on it, it is reported that the creation of that large water body had brought out greater problems for the preservation of these monuments. The increase of humidity due to great evaporation from the lake had increased erosion and wearing down of these monuments; also the higher rate of percolation of water from the lake is wearing down the foundation of the monuments at the new sites.

Inundation of natural resources: In Ghana, we at times pride ourselves for having created the largest man-made lake in the world. However, whether we should be happy or sad about this still remains to be seen. Considerable amount of land has been covered, the value of which to society and to the environment cannot be estimated in terms of present-day values alone. However, at least in terms of our present-day perceptions, before any such projects are undertaken the assessment of the impact of the dam construction on the environment must always include the estimate of the value of the land to be inundated in order to obtain a reasonably correct picture of the cost benefit ratio of the project.

Secondary salination: Normally, after construction of a dam in the upper reaches of a river, there is an accelerated formation of saline soils in the deltaic and tidal wave territories after periodic floodings have stopped (Kovda, 1978/1979). In general, if a dam is constructed in one or other part of the river basin, changes in the salt and silt in the deltaic and estuarine areas are unavoidable. Sometimes this secondary salination can spread several hundreds of kilometres from the point of the dam construction and gradually render the land infertile. In many places there has been the need to design appropriate techniques for watering, drainage and prevention of soil salination in the affected areas.

Underground Water Utilization: In recent times, there has been increased utilization of underground waters for water supply purposes in Ghana. There have also been several proposals for the use of underground water for irrigation. The Ghana Water and Sewerage Corporation on its own has completed over 2,500 boreholes across the country. Under the Canadian International Development Association (CIDA) programme (1974–81) another 2,500 boreholes have been drilled in the Upper East Region and Upper West Region which are very close to the Sahelian Region. And under Federal Republic of Germany's well-drilling programme (1978–83), 3,000 wells have been drilled in southern and central Ghana, giving a total of 8,000 boreholes in a country of about 238,280 km^2 The desire for the increased utilization of underground water is quite tremendous perhaps due to the fact that the construction and operation of such plants entail minimum cost compared to surface water plants. Such cost estimates can be related solely to the economy but certainly not to the environment. It is important, therefore, to bring to the notice of planners and deci-

93

sion makers, the problems likely to be associated with the pumping of underground waters in an environment such as ours in order to obtain the correct picture of how cost benefit analysis ought to be carried out. One such problem is the lowering of the water table generally. This may bring about rapid aridization with serious consequences for forestry and agriculture. With very erratic rainfall in this sub-region in recent times it would definitely be worthwhile to take a good look at this subject. In any case, there appears to be sufficient surface water in the country for us to leave underground waters alone.

Another problem which is also real in the country and which is associated with pumping underground water in coastal areas is the possible increase in salinity of underground waters in these regions where the underground waters are comparatively saline already (Table 13). Lowering the water table in these areas in relation to the sea as a result of pumping underground waters may bring about incursion of sea water into the underground waters resulting in increased salination which may affect top soils when the water table rises. In this way, most of the coastal soils might become salinated and barren in the very near future, with serious economic and ecological consequences.

There has also been suggestions from some quarters in the country for the use of comparatively saline underground waters in the coastal savannah for irrigation. One has to advise caution here for there is enough scientific evidence to show that even fresh water from rivers and lakes containing little amounts of salts gradually salinate irrigated soils (KOVDA, 1978/1979). May be it is time for us to stop planning for water as a unit and in isolation and to consider the management of water, forestry and land in an integrated way.

In countries like Canada from where we are obtaining technology and finance for the exploitation of underground water resources, underground water resources are plentiful (there is perennial underground water either from summer melted snow or from winter subglacial water bodies) and climatic conditions are far more stable. Moreover, Canada relies largely on underground water for water supply purposes since most surface water get frozen during winter. Their reliance on underground waters is, therefore, quite understandable. Countries in this sub-region

94

TABLE 13

Quality of Groundwater in the Accra Plains

Range of Concentrations (in mg/1 except pH) of Selected Parameter in Accra Plains (Near the Coast)			Range of Concentrations (in mg/1 except pH) of Selected Parameter At the Foothill of Akwapim Range (Further up from the Coast)		
Parameter	*Min.*	*Mean*	*Max.*	*Min.*	*Mean*	*Max.*
Chloride (Cl)	26	1074	7000	23.3	216	828
Iron (fe)	0.2	0.9	11.2	0.02	1.8	12.6
Sulphate (SO$_4$)	0.0	4.37	1,992	0.00	242	913
Total Disolved Solids (TDS)	130	2,856	14,584	49	640	2,210
Total Hardness	56	1,085	3,230	36	263	1,310
pH	60	7.3	9.1	5.5	6.8	7.98

Source: T. A. Amuzu 1979. *Quality of Ground Water in the Accra Plains.* Accra: WRRU, CSIR.

Note: Chloride and Sulphate concentrations in boreholes up country are hardly more than 100 mg/1 each (Data from Ghana Water and Sewerage Corporation).

where the Sahara desert is threatening to engulf a greater protion of the land, however, have to look quite seriously at their reliance on underground waters in view of its possible impact on the environment.

A statement made by Verhoog (1983) is worth noting. He said among other things that "until 1970, we took climate as something inherently stable with stochastic variations around the mean. Now we are not sure anymore. Nobody can prove any long-term climate or trend, but there certainly are large scale variations. In other words, climate is variable. The consequences of variability are not so pronounced in the temperate, middle latitudes and humid tropical regions, but it is very much so in the sub artic, Sahelian and semi arid zones. This is illustrated by the drought in the Sahel". He continues. "A very large part of the African region is very sensitive to climate variations as regards rainfall. This should mean that in those areas there should be adjustments to our scientific approach and also the general planning approaches. We should become more aware that our thinking is very much influenced by the results of research and approaches developed in the temperate climate, where climate variations have less impact".

In developing countries, therefore, those in charge of planning and technology transfer ought to be particularly careful because economic aid from most developed countries come in already tied up with marketable technology and facilities that might not be suitable to local environmental conditions. This certainly emphasizes the importance of environmental impact assessment in all development programmes, and also the need to maintain efficient monitoring systems in all areas of environmental operations for the effective appraisal of development strategies.

Chapter 7

INSTITUTIONAL ARRANGEMENTS AND MANPOWER NEEDS

The preceding chapters have dealt with various pollution problems and approaches to be adopted to bring them under control and to minimize them in development processes. This chapter looks at the institutional arrangements and manpower needs for effective management of activities that affect the environment.

Institutional Arrangements

In dealing with this topic one has to be aware of the fact that although the basic principles in pollution control and environmental protection in general are quite universal, no two nations can have the same institutional arrangement. The basis for variations in different countries are many and varied including the prevailing socio-economic conditions, the administrative and political structures and the state and nature of the environment itself. Generally speaking, however, there are two factors that influence the nature of institutional arrangements suitable for pollution control in any particular country. These are:

(1) How to deal with existing pollution problems.

(2) How to minimize pollution in the development processes.

Both factors have been discussed in the preceding chapters, but of the two the latter becomes much more important in developing countries where much lies ahead in terms of development. In this regard, environmental planning and natural resource management stand out clearly as the most important considerations. For it is through development that the environment is affected either positively or negatively and it is through management of development and resources that the environment could be well protected. It is in recognition of this that the second governing council of the UNEP, in 1974, resolved to emphasize institutional building at the national level in order to bring the problems under control worldwide.

The establishment of the Environmental Protection Council (EPC) of Ghana in 1974 was in line with this. The Council has, however, been experiencing teething problems since its establishment. Initially it was appropriately placed, or so I think, under the Ministry of Finance and Economic Planning where it was possible to have made an impact on the planning and development processes. However, its presence there was not seriously felt and in 1981 it was transferred to the Ministry of Health, and then again in 1982 to the Ministry of Local Government.

The establishment of the Council came at the time when the environmental wind was blowing over the whole world. Ghana was not unaffected by the fever, albeit largely in theory. However, Beal (1980) says, "a good theory does not necessarily get anything done practically. Practice is in the hands of the skilled manager, administrator and the legislative draftsman. If these people are given slogans and abstract philosophies to translate into purposeful action, only rhetoric will result. If on the other hand they have a clear idea of the kind of institutions they need to build, the linkages they need to forge between new and existing institutions, the technique and the tools available to them and the means by which they should be delivering the environmental goods, these same managers and administrators will be able to achieve the results their leaders call for".

In developing countries, it is essential that the environment office be considered as one of the most important institutions. This should be so because the need to adopt a total environmental planning approach to development is much more desirable in developing countries than elsewhere. The office must, therefore, be placed in a position where it is possible to oversee and to screen likely environmental consequences of development programmes at the planning stage and ensure compliance with the principle of environmental development. In other words, the office should be placed at the highest planning and decision-making level. It must be staffed with well-trained professionals who are capable of preparing national environmental policy guidelines for both planning and executing agencies to use in the appraisal of their own activities.

In theory, Ghana has all the institutions whose efforts might

98

bring about sound environmental development. In practice, however, the activities of the institutions are largely unco-ordinated. What normally happens among these organizations are duplication, inactivity, no man's land etc. In the area of liquid waste management, for example there are about five organizations controlling it, each operating independently. These organizations are the Ministry of Roads and Highways which constructs large concrete drains, the Ministry of Local Government which controls siltable natural waterways through the mosquito control unit, the city and urban councils which control small street drains, the State Housing Corporation which controls drainage in their estates, and the Ghana Water and Sewerage Corporation. Such unco-ordinated partnership has been a fertile ground for inefficient management. Perhaps what is required is for the EPC to assume the full role of the co-ordinating body assigned to it under Section 2 (i)(a) of the Act establishing it, and help streamline the activities of all the organizations operating in the environmental field. Under present conditions, it is extremely difficult to blame the various institutions for the present state of affairs. Conditions have been such that they have not been able to operate anywhere near their optimum levels of efficiency. It might, therefore, not be advisable to suggest radical changes in the present structures. With slight modifications, one would like to suggest the retention of the basic form but with massive injection of professionalism and efficiency into the system. It is also suggested that the environment office be placed under the Head of State or Head of Government, whoever holds the executive powers, with the following functions:

(1) Formulation of environmental policy within the framework of national development policy.
(2) Preparation of environmental legislation.
(3) Preparation of guidelines for planning, project implementation and natural resources management.
(4) Review and recommendation of environmental impact assessment (Impact assessment to be carried out by executing agencies).
(5) Monitoring of project implementation and operation to ensure compliance with environmental guidelines.
(6) Carrying out of environmental research into all areas of

99

environmental operation for constant review of environmental policy, recommendations and guidelines.

(7) Responsibility for pollution control including holding consultancy for all aspects of waste management.

(8) Preparation of annual report on the state of the environment.

(9) Environmental education.

With the above functions, the following structure (Fig. 13) is suggested for the office of the environment.

(1) There should be an inter-ministerial council on the environment to serve as the governing body of the office of the environment.

(2) There should be an office of the environment headed by a chief executive who should also be secretary to the inter-ministerial council.

(3) There should be inter-departmental consultative committee on the environment. This committee should be chaired by the chief executive of the office of the environment.

(4) The chief executive shall also be a member of the national planning commission.

(5) Under the chief executive, whose office (the secretariat) should comprise of finance, administration, public relations and legal sections, there should be three main departments.

   (a) Pollution Control Department to be responsible for pollution problems and to hold consultancy for all aspects of waste management.

   (b) Environmental Planning Department to be responsible for preparation of guidelines for planning and monitoring of project implementation and operation to ensure compliance with environmental guidelines.

   (c) Natural Resources Management Department to be responsible for the establishment of guidelines through inter-departmental consultative committee, for the management of natural resources: forestry, minerals, game and wildlife, parks and gardens etc. and to carry out climatic studies focussed on the study and use of surface and underground water.

An alternative to the above structural arrangements is to consider

100

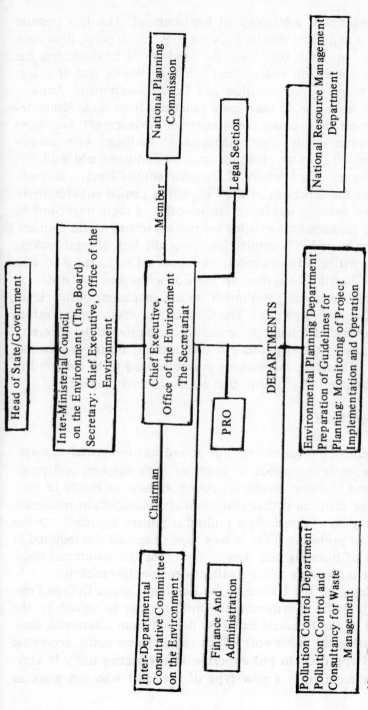

Note: There should be regional office headed by regional directors who report directly to the Chief Executive. The Regional Office should be structured along similar lines.

Fig. 13. Model structure for the Office of the Environment

Head of State/Government

Inter-Ministerial Council on the Environment (The Board)
Secretary: Chief Executive, Office of the Environment

National Planning Commission

Member

Legal Section

National Resource Management Department

Chief Executive,
Office of the Environment
The Secretariat

Chairman

PRO

DEPARTMENTS

Inter-Departmental Consultative Committee on the Environment

Finance And Administration

Environmental Planning Department
Preparation of Guidelines for Planning: Monitoring of Project Implementation and Operation

Pollution Control Department
Pollution Control and Consultancy for Waste Management

the setting up of a Ministry of Environment. This is a popular trend now and some developing countries, e.g. Nigeria, have such ministries. In some countries, the Ministry of Environment has absorbed some other Ministries such as Works and Housing, Transport and Communication and Local Government. Another approach would be to take some functions from these Ministries and assemble them under the Ministry of Environment. Functions such as water supply, waste management, drainage, water resources, town and country planning, forestry and game and wild life. In the absence of a Ministry of Environment in Ghana, it is considered that the functions of the EPC can be carried out effectively within the existing legislative framework and there might not be any need to amend the existing instrument setting up the Council. One often hears EPC complaining about the lack of legal backing for its activities. This can hardly be supported by facts for Section 17 of the instrument setting up the Council places the burden on the Council to advise government on the enactment of such legislations (See the Appendix). The Council's problem appears rather to be the lack of trained personnel who can provide the necessary data leading to the enactment of such legislation and who are also capable of charting the delicate course needed to be followed in the management of problems that affect the environment.

Manpower Needs

The manpower requirements for sound environmental management are quite enormous in terms of both numbers and proficiency, and in many developing countries they can hardly be met. The major problem is that environmental management requires a completely new approach, a multi-disciplinary approach, to the solution of problems. Thus, a new type of specialist is required in all areas of planning and development, for the traditional disciplines are inadequate to cope with environmental problems.

According to the University of London, Chelsea College Prospectus of 1976 "Environmental problems can be solved by the blending of the technical expertise derived from traditional disciplines within the framework which requires new social, economic and legal approach to put expertise into effective use". It says, "what is required is a new type of specialist who can work as part of a collaborative team of experts each of whom is trained to be aware of the overall nature of the environmental problem and also be able to identify how his own specialist skill can assist in the solution".

A survey of the Universities in Ghana and in many Universities in other developing countries shows that they have been slow in introducing environmental (multi-disciplinary) courses into their curricula. In places where this has been done, most institutions offer courses with curricula patterned after those of the industrialized countries and do not respond to local needs. Most countries also prefer sending such students to developed countries for training, most of whom do not return and the few who return become discontented with the system at home and thus become ineffective in their work.

The practice of looking for international technical assistance for the training of these new type of professionals in developing countries must give way to the training of these professionals locally. In this way, courses could be designed to suit local conditions. After all it is local problems that these people are getting trained to solve. As McGarry (1972) says "Apart from drawing the more educated manpower from the developing countries at substantial opportunity cost, the practice of sending students abroad for training has additional drawback for not supporting local educational programme". He says of sanitary engineers trained abroad "a student who should be acquiring training in overall waste management systems design end up studying such obscure topics as the production of polysaccharides by microbes involved in the activated sludge process". Topics like this satisfy the needs and operational requirements of the systems in operation in the developed countries but hardly that of the developing countries. This emphasizes the need for environmental courses to be organized locally for students to be exposed to the problems they will be dealing with after the completion of their courses.

In water pollution control, for example, students who undertake courses in Britain are aware of the most famous Royal Commission Standards of BOD 20 suspended solids 30. These standards are based on conditions peculiar to British and temperate environments. Among the conditions is the fact that the maximum temperature of the receiving water course does not exceed $20^{\circ}C$, the

103

maximum attainable in many temperate rivers. Time for the BOD test was also fixed at 5 days. This represents the maximum time taken by British rivers to flow from source to the open sea. These and other parameters such as the minimum dilution required were arrived at by conducting tests on British rivers which are naturally fast-flowing with high dissolved oxygen levels compared to most tropical rivers which are sluggish with maximum temperatures of more than 30°C.

The Royal Commission standards are, therefore, not directly applicable to tropical conditions. Also toxicological standards for the maintenance of water quality have been based largely on the salmonid in the temperate region. This fish does not occur in tropical fresh waters and as such the standards are not relevant to tropical situations.

It is necessary to point these out because with present level of understanding of the basic principles of pollution control in many developing countries, the tendency in these countries is to accept what obtains in the developed world as being universally applicable. An example is found with the United States decision to suspend or ban certain pesticides in the 1970s. This prompted similar actions by countries where environmental conditions are quite different. Usually countries with hot climates are confronted with serious pest problems unknown in the temperate regions. This factor creates greater demand for the use of pesticides in the hot climates. Moreover, environmental consideration may weigh less here since the degradation of active ingredients usually proceeds faster in hot climates. Experience has shown that in many developing countries, aroused but ill-informed public opinion at times insists that something be done to remedy a situation, and an industry or government body without the necessary know-how may be obliged to take a completely useless action so that it could be seen to be doing something; such an action may not only be wasteful of resources but may also be positively harmful to the socio-economic wellbeing of the people.

It should be realized by developing countries that learning through their mistakes is rather a costly way of building a society. They must, therefore, take their manpower training seriously and also restructure their institutions and management approaches to ensure that problems are handled efficiently at the planning and developmental stages in the interest of the long term socio-economic wellbeing of their people.

FUNCTIONS OF ENVIRONMENTAL PROTECTION COUNCIL
AS LAID DOWN IN THE
ENVIRONMENTAL PROTECTION COUNCIL
DECREE, 1974 NRCD 239

Establish-
ment of the
Environ-
mental
Protection
Council

In pursuance of the National Redemption Council (Establishment) Proclamation, 1972 this Decree is hereby made:—

1. There shall be established an Environmental Protection Council (in the Decree referred to as "the Council").

Functions
of the
Council

2. (1) The functions of the Council are:

(a) to advise the Government generally on all environmental matters relating to the social and economic life of Ghana.

(b) to co-ordinate the activities of all bodies concerned with environmental matters, and to serve as a channel of communication between these bodies and the Government.

(c) to conduct and promote investigations, studies, surveys, research and analyses, including the training of personnel, relating to the improvement of Ghana's environment and the maintenance of sound ecological system;

(d) to serve as the official national body for co-operating and liaising with national and international organizations on environmental matters;

(e) to undertake such studies and submit such reports and recommendations with respect to environmental matters as the Government may request;

(f) to embark upon general environmental educational programmes for the purpose of creating an enlightened public opinion regarding the environment and an awareness of the public's individual and collective role in its protection and improvement;

(g) without prejudice to the economic and social advancement of Ghana, to ensure the observance of proper safeguards in the planning and execution of all development projects, including those already in existence, that are likely to interfere with the quality of the environment;

(h) to perform such other functions as the Government may assign to the Council, or as are incidental or conducive to the exercise by the Council of all or any of the foregoing functions.

Other functions are found in Sections 15, 16, and 17.

Research and Records 15. The Council shall, with a view to facilitating present or future research or planning, maintain and preserve such records relating to its functions as it shall consider proper; and shall have power to engage in research in respect of any matter relating to those functions and to publish such records and the results of any research in which it may engage.

Annual Reports 16. The Council shall annually, not later than six months after the end of its financial year, prepare and submit to the Government a report on the activities of the Council during the preceding year.

Regulations 17. The Commissioner responsible for Economic Planning may, by legislative instrument, make such regulations on the recommendations of the Council, as the Commissioner may think fit for the purposes of giving full effect to the provisions of this Decree.

Transitional provision 18. The Chairman and officers of the Council holding office immediately before the commencement of this Decree shall be deemed to have been duly appointed under this Decree.

Commencement 19. This Decree shall be deemed to have come into force on the 1st day of September, 1973.

Projected Activities:

Some of the ways in which the EPC hopes to discharge its functions are as follows: —

(i) Creating an enlightened public opinion and awareness of environmental problems and the public's individual and collective role in its improvement and protection by using the radio and televion, the press, films, instructional material, compaigns, formal and informal education, symposia, conferences and seminars.

(ii) Undertaking research into environmental problems, laying emphasis on those of a pressing nature such as sanitation, the combating of environmental diseases such as river blindness, bilharzia, etc. In all these activities EPC works closely with various Ministries and Departments.

(iii) Setting standards of environmental quality to be observed by industry.

(iv) Advising Government and industry on the best ways of disposing of industrial wastes (solids and liquids) and gases likely to create

107

environmental hazards to humans, animals and plants.

(v) Advising on the most effective use of the country's natural resources.

(vi) Advising Government on legislation required for maintaining sound environmental standards. Several laws already exist, but many of these require updating and new ones are called for to meet the country's rapidly changing economic and social conditions.

(vii) Advising Government and private individual on how best any project can be set up so as to avoid the creation of environmental problems.

Issued by the public relations office of the EPC 15th June, 1979.

Author's Note:

With the exception (i) above not much has been achieved in the other areas.

REFERENCES

Amuzu T. A. 1979. *Quality of Groundwater in the Accra Plains*. Accra: Water Resources Research Unit, Council for Scientific and Industrial Research.

Ayibontele, Nii Boi and Tufour-Darko, T. 1979. *Sediment Load of Southern Rivers of Ghana*. Accra: Water Resources Research Unit, Council for Scientific and Industrial Research.

Beal, J.C. 1980. *The Manager and the Environment*. London: Pergamon Press.

Berg, K. *et al.* 1958. Furesoundersogelser 1950–54. *Folia Limnologica Scandinavica* 10, 189pp.

Ben-Dyke, R., Sanderson, D. M. and Noakes D.N. 1970. Acute toxicity data for pesticides. *World Review of Pest Control* 9:119–127.

Bolton, R. and Klein, L. 1971. *Sewage Treatment Basic Principles and Trends*, 2nd ed. London Butterworths.

Brooker, M. P. and Edwards, R. W. 1975. Aquatic herbicides and the control of water weeds. *Water Research.* 9: 1–15.

Buckley, A. D. 1974. Estuarial and coastal pollution. *Journal of Water Pollution Control* 1974: 307–320.

Buggler, Jeremy 1972. *Polluting Britain*. London: Penguin Books Ltd.

Cole, E. A. 1941. The effect of pollutional waste on life. In *A Symposium on Hydrobiology Madison*, pp. 47–57.

Commoner, Barry 1972. *The Closing Circle*. Washington, D.C. Jonathan Cape.

Danso, J.K. 1986. Environmental management of aluminium smelting industry in Ghana. *UNEP/1 PA 1 Multi-Regional Workshop, Dubai.*

Doxiadis Associates Ltd. 1962. *ATMA Master Plan Tema Ghana.*

Environmental Protection Council Decree, 1974 (NRCD 239). Accra: Ghana Publishing Corporation.

Factories Officers and Shops Act 328, 1979. Accra: Ghana Publishing Corporation.

FOA/UNDP 1971. *Volta Lake Research Ghana Interim Report.* Rome.

Ghana Water and Sewerage Act 310, 1965. Accra: Ghana Publishing Corporation.

Ghana Water and Sewerage Regulations, 1979 (LI 1233). Accra: Ghana Publishing Corporation.

Ghana Urban Development Project. Vol 2 *Nima Maamobi*, 1977, Huzzar Brammah and Associates – Roger Tym and Associates – Allott Lomax Ministry of Works and Housing.

Goodman, G. T. 1974. How do chemical substances affect the environment. In *Proceedings of the Royal Society of London* Series B, 185: 127–148.

Hammerton, G. 1955. Observations on the decay of synthetic detergents in natural water. *Journal of Applied Chemistry* 5.

Hynes, H.B.N. 1974. *Biology of Polluted Waters*. Liverpool: Liverpool University Press.

Imhoff, K. 1955. The final step in sewage treatment. *Sewerage Industrial Waters* 27: 332–335.

109

Jopp, Keith 1965. *Volta: the Story of Ghana's Volta River Project.* Accra: VRA.

Klein, L. 1957. *Aspects of River Pollution.* London: Butterworths Scientific Publications.

Kovda, V.A. 1978/1979. *Problems of Combating Salinization of Irrigated Soils* (Selected Lectures). UNEP, GKNT, USSR.

Larsen, K. and Olsen, S. (1950). Ochre suffocation of fish in River Tim. *Annual Report of the Danish Biological Station* 50: 5–27.

Lumis, Eric T.B. 1976. *Environmental Policy and Law.* London: UK Department of Environment.

Mackenthun, K.M., Herman, E.F. and Bartsch, A.F. 1945. A heavy mortality of fishes resulting from the decomposition of algae in the Yahara River. *Transactions of the American Fisheries Society* 75: 175–180.

MacGarry, Michael G. 1978. *Water Wastes and Health in Hot Climates.* Chichester: John Wiley and Sons Ltd.

Mensah, Getrude 1976. *Water Quality and Pollution Survey of Inland and Coastal Waters of Ghana.* Accra: Water Resources Research Unit, Council of Scientific and Industrial Research.

Paul, R.M. 1952. Water pollution: a factor modifying fish population in Pacific Coast. *Streams Science* 74, 114–117.

Pearsall, W.H., Gardiner, A.C. and Greenshilds, F. 1946. Fresh water biology and water supply in Britain. *Scientific Publication. Fresh Water Biological Association.* 11, 90pp.

Pentelow, F.T.K. 1949. Fisheries and pollution from china clay works. *Report on Salmon and Freshwater Fisheries, London,* 31, 4pp.

Public Health (Drainage of Trade Premises) Act, 1937. London: Her Majesty's Stationery Stores.

Public Health (Removal of Night Soil) Act, 1975. Accra: Ghana Publishing Corporation.

Redeke, H.C. 1927. Report on the pollution of rivers and its relation to fisheries. *Rapp. Cons. Explor. Mer.* 43: 1–50.

Ricci, Paslo F. 1985. Regulating cancer risks. *Environmental Science and Technology,* 19 (6): 473–479.

The Rivers (Prevention of Pollution) Act, 1951. London: Her Majesty's Stationery Stores.

Royston, Michael G. 1979. *Pollution Prevention Pays.* Oxford: Pergamon Press.

The Rivers (Precention and Pollution) Act, 1876. London: Her Majesty's Stationery Stores.

Tahal Consulting Engineers Ltd., Tel Avivi, Israel 1981. *Accra–Tema Water Supply and Sewerage Project, Review of Master Plan Final Report,* Vol. 1 and 2.

Thomas, G.W. 1970 Soil and climatic factors which affect nutrient mobility. In *Nutrient Mobility in Soils; Accumulation and Losses* (ed. O.O. Engelstall). Soil Science Society of America Special Publication.

Turing, H.D. 1947–9. *Four Reports on Pollution affecting Rivers in England,*

Wales and Scotland. London: British Field Sport Society.

UN 1974. *Report of the World Food Conference Rome 5 – 16 November, 1974.* UN Publication Sales No. E. 75. 11. A.3.

UN 1983. *Formulation of Pesticides in Developing Countries.* UN Publication Sales No. E. 83 11. B.B. 01550p.

The Water Act, 1973. London: Her Majesty's Stationery Stores.

Verhoog, F. 1983. *Report of the Sub-Regional Workshop on the Water Resources of the Volta Basin, Accra 1983.*

Wuhrmann, K. and Woker, H. 1958. Vergiftugen der aquatischen Fauna durch Gewasserverunreiningungen. *Verhandlungen der Internationales Vereinigung für theorstiche und angewandte Limnologie* 13, 557–583.

INDEX

112

114

116